THE RIVER COLUMN

THE RIVER COLUMN

A NARRATIVE OF THE ADVANCE
OF THE RIVER COLUMN OF THE
NILE EXPEDITIONARY FORCE,
AND ITS RETURN DOWN
THE RAPIDS

BY

Major-General Henry Brackenbury, C.B.

WITH MAPS
by Major The Hon. F. L. L. Colborne

The Naval & Military Press Ltd

Reproduced by kind permission of the Central Library,
Royal Military Academy, Sandhurst

Published by
The Naval & Military Press Ltd
Unit 10, Ridgewood Industrial Park,
Uckfield, East Sussex,
TN22 5QE England
Tel: +44 (0) 1825 749494
Fax: +44 (0) 1825 765701
www.naval-military-press.com

© The Naval & Military Press Ltd 2005

In reprinting in facsimile from the original, any imperfections are inevitably reproduced and the quality may fall short of modern type and cartographic standards.

PREFACE.

I HAVE written this simple narrative in the belief that the advance and return of four regiments of infantry through a hundred miles of cataracts and rapids in an enemy's country deserve, as a military operation, some permanent record, and because death has removed the only other officers possessing sufficient knowledge of all details to write that record with accuracy.

It would have been a pleasure to me to take this opportunity of praising those individuals to whom, in my opinion, such success as the Column attained is chiefly due;

but my position demands so strict a neutrality that I have thought it right to avoid all words of praise, lest in any case their accidental omission might appear to impute the semblance of blame.

HENRY BRACKENBURY.

LONDON, *September* 1885.

CONTENTS.

CHAP.		PAGE
I.	KORTI TO MERAWI—ADVANCED GUARD,	1
II.	MERAWI TO HAMDAB—ADVANCED POST,	21
III.	HAMDAB—ORGANISATION,	39
IV.	HAMDAB—CONCENTRATION,	54
V.	HAMDAB TO KAB EL ABD—TOUCH OF THE ENEMY,	73
VI.	KAB EL ABD TO GAMRA — RETREAT OF THE ENEMY,	88
VII.	BIRTI—HALT, AND ADVANCE OF THE ENEMY,	107
VIII.	KIRBEKAN—RECONNAISSANCE AND PREPARATION,	136
IX.	KIRBEKAN—THE FIGHT,	152
X.	THE SHUKOOK PASS,	172
XI.	SALAMAT — DESTRUCTION OF SULEIMAN WAD GAMR'S PROPERTY,	197
XII.	HEBBEH—THE PASSAGE OF THE NILE,	211
XIII.	HEBBEH—THE SCENE OF COLONEL STEWART'S MURDER,	224
XIV.	HUELLA—THE END OF THE MONASSIR COUNTRY,	234
XV.	RECALL—BACK TO SALAMAT,	246
XVI.	RUNNING THE RAPIDS—BACK TO HAMDAB,	265
XVII.	THE BREAK-UP OF THE COLUMN—BACK TO KORTI,	285

LIST OF MAPS.

	PAGE
SKETCH OF GROUND AT KIRBEKAN, . . .	170
SKETCH OF RIVER NILE AT HEBBEH, . .	232
SKETCH OF RIVER NILE, FROM MERAWI TO HUELLA, ...	*At end*

THE RIVER COLUMN.

CHAPTER I.

KORTI TO MERAWI—ADVANCED GUARD.

On the morning of the 24th December 1884, I arrived at Korti, Lord Wolseley's headquarters—having up to that time been engaged as Deputy Adjutant and Quartermaster General under General Sir Redvers Buller, the chief of the staff, in the organisation of the Nile Expedition. The exact nature of Lord Wolseley's plans was not at that time known to me; but I knew that his original idea of moving the whole force by river to Berber and thence to Khartoum had necessarily to be abandoned, and that, if Gordon were to be rescued within the period we had reason to hope he could hold out for, troops must be sent across the desert. That this was a more or less desperate venture, none of us could for a moment doubt; but it had to be made, if Gordon were to be saved; and in the four camel regiments, camel battery, camel-bearer company, camel field-hospital, and camel transport-companies, a force had been specially organised for this effort. It was not, however, till after General Buller's arrival at Korti, that the exact nature of Lord Wolseley's plan was made known to me, and the details of the scheme had then to be worked out.

The plan, in its bare outline, was as follows: The greater portion of the mounted troops, under Sir Herbert Stewart, was to advance across the desert from Korti to Metemmeh, establishing fortified posts at the wells along the route. Sir Charles Wilson was then, with a small escort of infantry, to proceed in Gordon's steamers to Khartoum, and, having communicated with Gordon, to return to Metemmeh. Upon his report the future conduct of the desert column would be framed. I do not know what instructions Sir Herbert Stewart may have received; but I do know that if Stewart had not been killed, and if Wilson had brought back word that Gordon was holding out, but in sore need, Stewart and the troops under him were capable of forcing their way to Gordon's assistance through any number of the enemy. And I know that if Wilson's report as to Gordon's power of holding out had been favourable, Lord Wolseley himself had intended to join Stewart, taking with him the remainder of the mounted troops and a force of infantry.

Simultaneously with the advance of the desert column under Stewart, a force was to be sent by river under command of General Earle to punish the murderers of Colonel Stewart and of the Consuls, and to advance by Berber to co-operate with Stewart's force in an attack on the Mahdi before Khartoum, under Lord Wolseley's personal command.

I was informed that Lord Wolseley had selected me to be second in command of this column and chief staff-officer to Major-General Earle ; and on Christmas Day General Buller set me free from my work in his office—bringing in Colonel Wolseley, A.A.G., to replace me—and told me to devote my whole time to organising General Earle's column, as Lord Wolseley wanted me to proceed at the earliest possible date with a battalion of infantry and a few cavalry to establish an advanced post at Hamdab, above the portion of river marked in the map as the Gerendid cataract, and near the point (Dugiyet) where the desert road from Berber strikes the river. General Earle was at this time at Dongola.

I had some few details to discuss with Herbert Stewart. The cavalry of the expedition—five troops—was to be evenly divided between us; and the Royal Engineers, who had reached Korti in boats, were, with their equipment, to be divided into two portions—one to accompany the desert and one the river column. We had no difficulty in settling matters amicably.

The first battalion of the South Staffordshire Regiment—the battalion which had first ascended the river in whalers—was to lead the advance up the river. I had accompanied them on their start from Gemai dockyard, above the second cataract, to Sarras; and had congratulated Colonel Eyre upon the strange chance which had given him, as the boat at the head of his column, that bearing the number 38, the old number of his regiment; and knowing what a keen soldier he was, I was glad to have him with me now.[1]

In making the preparations for a start, it

[1] Another curious coincidence was the fact that the first boat taken up through the great gate of the second cataract, under the superintendence of Colonel Butler, bore the number 69—the number of his old regiment, of whose "Records" he is the historian.

was found that the original liberal allowance of boat-gear with which the troops had started had been sadly reduced by the journey up the river, and that we could not count upon more than eight oars and two poles per boat. And as the supplies of food brought up by the Staffords were being taken in great quantities for the desert column, we had to content ourselves with thirty days' boat rations for the present. In a memo. written to Colonel Eyre on the 26th, authorising an issue of soap, I said : " In this and every similar issue, you must impress upon your men the necessity of economy. They have many weeks, probably some months, of work yet before them, and all supplies are limited in quantity."

At this time Colonel Colvile was at Merawi, or rather at Abu Dom, which is to Merawi what Southwark is to London. With him was the Vakeel of the Mudirieh of Dongola, Gaudet Bey, with some 400 of the Mudir's troops. The Mudir was supposed to be collecting supplies for us; and

I entered into telegraphic correspondence with Colonel Colvile, telling him the quantities of barley, dourra, dourra-stalk, and firewood we required to be ready for us on our arrival.

On Sunday, the 28th December, at 2 P.M., the Staffords, 545 of all ranks, entered their fifty boats. I had issued orders previously to the following effect: "From the time of leaving Korti, the company will be the unit by which boats will work. The utmost efforts must be made to keep companies together. In every case an officer will be with the last boat of the company, and it will be his duty to urge on, and assist where necessary, any boats of his company which may be falling behind." Working on this principle, the Staffords started, and in thirty-one minutes their last boat was under way. It was the first time that a whole battalion had moved together, and as it was the first forward movement beyond Korti, it was full of interest. Two boats, containing a detachment, 26th Company,

28th Dec.

R.E., under Captain Blackburn, left at the same time.

9th Dec. Early on the 29th half a troop of 19th Hussars, under Captain Aylmer, twenty-six of all ranks, and thirty horses, marched to overtake the Staffords, taking with them the horses and camels of my own party; and in the afternoon I started in the Monarch steam-launch with Major Slade, D.A.A.G., Intelligence Department; Captain Beaumont, K.R.R., officer for signalling; and D.A.C.G. Boyd, of the Commissariat.

Before starting I said good-bye to two old friends whom I was never destined to see again, Herbert Stewart and St Leger Herbert. We had all served together in South Africa, and at the storming of Sekukuni's fighting koppie. We had lived together and travelled together for many a weary league. Stewart had succeeded me as military secretary to Lord Wolseley when I went to join the Viceroy's staff in India. St Leger Herbert had been my companion on the staff in Cyprus as well. I do not know which was the keener soldier of the two. If ever a man loved fighting, it was St Leger Herbert; and Stewart's and my last words together were the mutually expressed hope that each of us would meet the enemy in force, and make an end of it in one good fight.

At 5 P.M. we overtook the Staffords and Hussars about twenty miles from Korti, and bivouacked for the night on the left bank at the village of Kureir, opposite Hanneck.

The following morning, 30th, we advanced to Abu Dom. Having selected a site for our bivouac, about half a mile above a strong fort that had been built by native labourers on the designs of the Vakeel, and below which the native troops were hutted, I visited Colonel Colvile, who was living in a grass hut on the river-bank close to the landing-place, surrounded by groaning camels and by natives anxious to bargain, or clamouring for payment for supplies or camels purchased for the desert column.

I now held an interview in Colonel Col-

_{30th Dec.}

vile's hut with the Vakeel, who was living on board a dahabeeyah close by, at which interview the Turkish major commanding the troops assisted. I told them our wants in the matter of supplies. Many difficulties were made, but ultimately all we wanted was promised, both in cattle, dourra, dourra-stalk, wood, and wheat, The exceptions were barley and flour—the Vakeel assuring me that the first was not in existence, and the latter not to be obtained in any large quantities, owing to the scarcity of grindstones. This we found to be true: there were only two large grindstones, of the kind which are turned one upon the other, in all the district; the flour for the use of each family being made by the women of the family, by pounding or rubbing with a stone a small handful at a time of wheat or dourra placed in a hollowed-out stone. The result of the interview, in spite of all promises, left on my mind the conviction that Gaudet Bey and the Major meant to be obstructive, and had no intention of doing for us any more than they could help; and I gave the Vakeel to understand that we must have what we wanted, and that the military commander must now reign supreme.

Colvile, Slade, and I then proceeded up the river in the picket-boat, with a view to selecting a camping-ground at Belal; but, finding we should not have time to get so far, we returned to Abu Dom. Immediately on our return we were informed that a messenger from Gordon had arrived, and that the Vakeel had telegraphed the fact to the Mudir. As this was in direct opposition to the instructions given by me in the morning, that no telegrams were to be sent unless first submitted to Colonel Colvile, I sent for the Vakeel; and on my saying I must report him to Lord Wolseley, he replied that he did not care—he was not Lord Wolseley's Vakeel. As I found that he had not collected the supplies which he had promised to collect on the opposite bank for our troops, and had replied, when asked about it, that he had not time to discuss the matter, I telegraphed to General Buller that I thought we should do better to send the Vakeel away, and appoint the Kasheef of Belal, Mohammed Effendi Wad Kenaish, to act in his place. The same night I received a telegram from General Buller saying that a very civil message had been sent to the Vakeel requesting him to come to Korti, and one from Sir C. Wilson, asking me to tell the Vakeel that Lord Wolseley wished to consult him on matters of importance, and begged he would go there by the picket-boat next day.

I then saw the messenger from Gordon. He was a man who had been sent by Colvile with a letter from Lord Wolseley; and he brought back that now historical letter of three words, " Khartoum all right, 14th December, C. G. Gordon." He told me that when he left Khartoum all was well there, and that provisions were sufficient, though not plentiful. On his way back he had remained six days in the Mahdi's camp.

Sickness was prevalent among the enemy, but there was no lack of food. He told me that Hashm el Moos was at Wady Bishara on the 21st December with three steamers, having loaded two steamers with provisions and sent them to Khartoum. He then added in great secrecy that Gordon had confided to him a message that we were to come quickly,—not to divide our force or leave Berber behind, but to take Berber and come by the right bank.

That night of bivouac was rendered hideous by the Mudir's troops. They had a semicircle of sentries from the fort to the river enclosing their huts and Colvile's camels; and they shouted the equivalent of "all's well" without cessation. Each sentry had a number, and as soon as No. 1 had called out "No. 1, all's well," No. 2 shouted "No. 2, all's well," and so on till the last number was reached, when No. 1 began again. This continued through the whole night. Colvile was used to it, and did not mind.

31st Dec. On the morning of the 31st the Vakeel and Gordon's messenger went off together to Korti in the Monarch picket-boat, Lieutenant Tyler, R.N., who was in charge, having great difficulty in carrying out his orders to keep them apart. I informed General Buller that I had appointed Mohammed Wad Kenaish to act in the Vakeel's place, instead of the major whom the Vakeel had named; and was instructed in reply that I should have accepted the deputy appointed by the Vakeel, and that my action amounted to taking the government of the country into our hands, which was not desirable. It was proposed to admonish the Vakeel seriously, and send him back. I urged by telegraph his not being sent back; but was informed that it would not do to start in one portion of the Mudirieh a policy different from that prevailing elsewhere. I vainly represented that part of this portion of the Mudirieh was in rebellion, and taxes could not be collected; that the Vakeel confessed himself unable to

ADVANCED GUARD.

punish the persons who cut the telegraph; that, according to the Vakeel, El Zain, with some of the Mahdi's dervishes, was at Hamdab, and that these were reasons why the military authority should be paramount here. I only found that I was uselessly kicking against the pricks. Lord Wolseley did not consider any of my reasons sufficient, and I was told the Vakeel would be sent back with General Earle.[1]

Meanwhile, throughout the day the Staffords with their boats had been employed in bringing over to the left bank the supplies collected in the Shoona or Government store on the right bank. Had I passed on, leaving the supplies in the Shoona, the bringing them over to the left bank might have been indefinitely postponed; and in the present temper of the Mudir's authorities, I did not feel sure the supplies would ever reach us. I considered it important to show that we meant

[1] The Vakeel afterwards told Colonel Colvile and myself that he was at this time acting under orders from the Mudir of Dongola to give us as little help as possible.

to have what we wanted, and were capable of helping ourselves, if need be; and this action had an undoubtedly good effect.

In the course of the day I presented Said Hassan, the Sheikh of Amri Island and King of Zowarah, with a robe of honour in Lord Wolseley's name. This monarch had joined the Shagiyeh in rebellion against the Egyptians in the previous summer, and had been badly wounded in the arm when fighting against the Mudir's troops at Korti. He had since thought better of it; and when, shortly before, Suleiman Wad Gamr had sent to his island to bring him to Birti, he had, according to his own story, escaped and fled to us. This noble conduct I had been instructed to reward in what was certainly a conspicuous manner; for when the old gentleman was clothed in a scarlet cloth robe, a crimson fez, a sword very much gilt with sundry gorgeous tassels, and a pair of red slippers, he was as like a monkey on a barrel-organ as anything I ever saw. But he was a king, and the act I had been performing was one with which every reader of the Scriptures is familiar. King Said's first act was to beg for money for himself and his ragged retinue, and to try to drive as hard a bargain with me as he could. I promised him finally a pound a-day for himself and his followers, provided he would help us with labour and supplies when we reached his country—payment to be contingent on results. He never was of the slightest use to us; and as, when we returned to Abu Dom, he did not hesitate to return among the rebels, I have little doubt that he had only followed the traditionary policy of the Soudanese sheikhs, to have some of a family on each side in a war, so that, whichever side wins, there may be some in power to intercede for those on the beaten side. In fact, so well is this policy recognised among them, that the members of the family who have been on the wrong side are thought none the worse of for their apparent treason.

About seven o'clock in the evening, telegraphic communication with Korti was interrupted. I did not learn this till nearly nine, and then at once sent out an officer of Engineers with a few Hussars and a native linesman to repair the line. They returned about 2.30 A.M., having found it cut about eight miles from our camp, and traces of camels leading into the desert. They had repaired the line.

<small>1st Jan. 1885.</small>

On New Year's Day the Staffords continued and completed the work of bringing over the supplies from the Shoona; and I rode with Major Slade and Captain Beaumont about eight miles, to Belal, at the foot of the Gerendid cataract, and selected a bivouac. On the way we passed close to a remarkable cluster of pyramids, many of which have crumbled away into gravel mounds, a few retaining their pyramidal form. Their bases are buried, but not deep, in the sand, and the highest stands about sixty feet above the present level. They stand in irregular rows. They are made of blocks of pudding-stone, of which there is a large quantity in the neighbourhood, faced with one layer of blocks of sandstone. No native has the vaguest idea of their age. They are undoubtedly tombs; their neighbourhood has been used as a graveyard from time immemorial, and is so now. I inquired at Belal if any curiosities, scarabæi, clay figures, or antiquities of any sort were ever found there, offering to purchase them at a good price; but was assured nothing had ever been found. On the opposite bank of the river, about equally distant from its present bed, stands another cluster of similar pyramids near the hill known as Jebel Barkal, in which a temple is hewn.

On New Year's night we dined outside Colonel Colvile's hut. In addition to the *menu* furnished by our rations, we had eggs and chickens, pumpkin, and a plum-pudding, a most delicious melon, a bottle of champagne, and a tot of whisky. The English mail arrived bringing us letters and Christmas cards, and we sat up till late, speculating on what the year would bring forth. Then saying good-bye to Colvile, we of the river column sought our beds on the soft, clean, yellow sand by the side of the sleeping troops.

CHAPTER II.

MERAWI TO HAMDAB—ADVANCED POST.

On the morning of the 2d, at six o'clock, 2d Jan. the Staffords moved off in their boats, the Hussars covering the advance along the bank. They arrived at Belal in the afternoon. Slade, with an escort, rode over to Hamdab to select a camping-ground for our concentration; the rest of our party remained at Belal. The Kasheef, Mohammed Wad Kenaish, brought us excellent wheaten cakes, honey, and melons, with milk both sweet and sour, in which latter condition only the natives seem to drink it. The people brought dates and milk and bread for sale to the troops.

Slade received information that there

were about 600 rebels at Birti, under Moussa, the son of Abu Hegel, sheikh of the Robatab tribe. Moussa, it was reported, had been made an Emir by the Mahdi, and was anxious to advance towards Hamdab. Suleiman Wad Gamr, sheikh of the Monassir tribe, was said to have objected to this advance, and to have left Birti on the 29th December with the intention of proceeding to Berber, and reporting the matter to Mohammed el Kheir, the Mahdi's Emir of Berber.

We also learnt the particulars of a raid which had been made much nearer to us on the last day of the year, and of which we had received information at Abu Dom. El Zain, a well known robber chief, with forty followers, had raided from the wells of El Koua, thirty miles out on the road from Dugiyet to Berber, and had captured nearly 200 camels which were grazing in the desert about two hours' march from the river. A large number of these camels belonged to the Kasheef of Belal.

We were now, it appeared, really beginning to approach a hostile country. Thirty miles in front of us was a force of Monassir and Robatab ready to fight, under a commander who wanted to lead them on; and thirty miles on our right flank was a famous raider with a number of followers more bold than numerous. We had been so long sitting still without a prospect of a fight, that we had begun almost to disbelieve in the possibility of one; but our prospects were apparently brightening.

We had a pleasant enough spot for our bivouac, with good anchorage, and a grove of palm-trees close by. But we noticed that the desert had now become rocky, and the rocks came close down to the river. The fine open sandy plain, so favourable for the development of modern infantry fire, so fatal to the Arab rush, had disappeared. We had entered into the region of rocks and cataracts, that we were to carry with us almost to the furthest limits of the country of the Monassir.

On the 3d we again advanced, our lead- 3d Jan.

ing boats reaching their camping-ground at Hamdab at one o'clock, and the last boat closing up to them by two; and this in spite of Omar, the sheikh of Duaim, whom we had chartered as a pilot, running Colonel Eyre's boat on a rock. We found no cataract, only a very rapid stream between rocks, against which the men were able to row. And so the Gerendid cataract,[1] of which we had a picture in the Intelligence Department publications, did not exist; and we began to congratulate ourselves on the prospect of an easy ascent to Berber.

News reached us that a party of fifty dervishes (the generic name for the Mahdi's followers, dressed in his patchwork uniform) was on the right bank opposite Ooli Island; and that El Zain at El Koua had been reinforced by forty men from Berber. We were now beyond Dugiyet, and the point, marked by a solitary dom-palm, where the chief desert-track from Berber strikes the

---

[1] No native of the district had ever heard this name. The local name is the rapids of Hajar Oolad Gurbar.

Nile. Under these circumstances the wells of El Koua and Bir Sani became an important point for our consideration, as the raid made towards the river might at any time be repeated, and our convoys from Abu Dom, of which the first arrived to-day, might be molested. But my handful of cavalry was too small to attempt any counterstroke in that direction, and I telegraphed to Korti asking for more cavalry, and expressing the desire that the Mudir's troops, whom I had been directed not to move, should cross the river, and encamp on the opposite bank to us, so as to prevent small parties of dervishes, such as we were informed were near Ooli Island, firing across the river into our camp at night.

Not liking the camp selected by Slade, 4th Jan. I rode out on the morning of the 4th and chose another site about a mile farther up stream, with good anchorage, and an excellent position for a small defensive work, on the site of an old mud fort placed on a rocky spur jutting out into the Nile, and commanding the river and the camp. We then rode on to Jebel Kulgeili, about five miles to the front, and ascended the mountain. From it we could see for many miles in every direction; but only about three miles of actual river were visible beyond the mountain, as the islands overlap and close the view near Ooli Island. We could see enough, however, to assure us that there was nothing to stop the boats' progress from Hamdab to Ooli.

As far as Belal we had been travelling through a rich country with much cultivation; at Belal, as already stated, the rocks came down to near the river, and from Belal to Hamdab but little cultivation existed. Beyond Hamdab the amount of cultivation still further diminished, and the people, who up to Hamdab had been friendly, became more shy, several houses being deserted. But from Kulgeili to Ooli there was not a sign of life. One or two strips of neglected cultivation existed, but every hovel was deserted. Hamdab marked the limits of territory within which the Mudir had collected taxes since the rebellion began; and those beyond that limit, not having paid taxes, had doubtless guilty consciences, and the fear bred thereof. We read, however, to those of them whom we could assemble between Belal and Kulgeili, Lord Wolseley's proclamation of friendliness to the Shagiyeh, and left copies of it with them.

In the afternoon General Earle arrived with his aide-de-camp, Lieut. St Aubyn, and Brigade-Major, Major Boyle, and assumed command. He brought with him Lord Wolseley's instructions, which had been shown to me before leaving Korti. In them he was informed that his force was to consist of—

>One squadron 19th Hussars;
>The Staffordshire Regiment;
>The Royal Highlanders;
>The Duke of Cornwall's Light Infantry;
>The Gordon Highlanders;
>A battery of Egyptian Artillery;
>The Egyptian Camel Corps;

Headquarters and 300 camels of the 11th Transport Company;
and that in addition another regiment would be placed at his disposal to form posts between Merawi and Abu Hamed. He was to concentrate at Abu Hamed, and advance thence as soon as he had collected a hundred days' supplies per man. Major Rundle, who had a large quantity of rations at Korosko, had undertaken to have a convoy of supplies at Abu Hamed four days after General Earle's arrival there. After filling up with supplies at Abu Hamed, General Earle was to advance upon Berber; and having secured that place, to endeavour to forward as many supplies as possible to the force which would have proceeded by land to Khartoum. A portion of the Mudir's troops was told off to accompany General Earle's force. He might use them as he thought fit, but it was suggested he should employ them to collect supplies in the Monassir country. He was to treat all tribes as friends (except the Monassir) if

they would meet his advances; if not, he was to enforce his demands. The Monassir were only to be treated as friends if they would give up the murderers of Colonel Stewart and his party. He was to occupy Abu Hamed and Berber, and such other places as might be necessary for the safety of his line; and to consider it of first importance to place 75,000 rations at Shendy at the disposal of the force operating by the desert as quickly as possible.

To the above military instructions some political instructions were added for General Earle in his dealings with the various tribes. The sheikhs, he was told, might be informed that the English policy was, in the first place, to restore peace and tranquillity to the country, and then to establish some form of native government which would be acceptable to the people. The English Government did not intend to interfere with the property or just rights of any one. All persons wishing to submit, with the exception of the murderers of Colonel

Stewart and his party, and their accomplices, would be well received and pardoned if they gave in their submission at once; but those persisting in rebellion would receive the punishment they deserved.

For the better carrying out of these instructions, letters in Arabic, addressed to the sheikhs of the various tribes, had been prepared; and General Earle was instructed, before entering each district, to send one of these letters to the sheikh or tribe to whom it was addressed. A special proclamation, offering a reward for the apprehension of Suleiman Wad Gamr and Fakri Wad Etman, the instigator and perpetrator of Stewart's murder, was to be circulated only when it should be known that Suleiman Wad Gamr had fled.

In the course of the afternoon a telegram arrived, instructing the General that he was not to advance beyond Hamdab until he could do so with his whole force. Lord Wolseley also wished him to avoid reconnaissances as much as possible,—deprecating reconnaissances from a stationary force, as the reconnoitrers must in the end retire to their force, and such a retirement is often magnified by natives into a defeat; and as it was of importance to prevent any opening being given for such a rumour.

On the 5th January Major Flood marched into camp with a troop and a half of Hussars, completing the squadron to 91 sabres; and the troops were employed preparing the newly selected camp. We were now nineteen miles from the telegraph station at Abu Dom; but there was lying along the ground between us, and in the river at Merawi, much wire belonging to the old Berber line, which had crossed the desert from Dugiyet, and Lieutenant Stuart, R.E., was already at work getting poles cut and erected by native labour. Meanwhile we had established a daily camel-post with Abu Dom; and to-day we received by it the welcome news from General Buller that Herbert Stewart had successfully established posts at Gakdul and Howeiyet, had

5th Jan.

found plenty of water, grass, and firewood, and would return with the convoy to-day. His expedition to Gakdul, we were told, had been a complete surprise. No opposition had been offered, and he had captured several prisoners.

6th Jan. On the 6th, in a most unpleasant duststorm, the troops moved into their new camp. A market was at once established; and the natives brought in a fair supply of milk, dates, dourra-bread, and other products of the country. So well satisfied with our treatment of them were the natives, that several of them afterwards followed us up the country, bringing dates to sell. Three of these met with their death at the hands of some Monassir, near Kirbekan, a few days after the action there.

The daily record from this date to the 23d January would have but little general interest. The troops for the column continued to arrive at Abu Dom and Hamdab; and we were busily occupied in perfecting our arrangements for the advance.

The organisation of our force necessitated my making one trip to Korti, and several to Abu Dom; and General Earle had to go once to Abu Dom to bring the Vakeel to book. Of that organisation I propose to speak in the next chapter.

Only one or two matters of external interest occurred during this period. The sheikh of Ooli, or rather a younger brother of the sheikh, stating that the sheikh was lame and unable to walk, came into our camp and asked for the protection promised under Lord Wolseley's proclamation to the Shagiyeh. This he was promised on condition that he helped us to obtain supplies.

At 1.45 A.M. on the 13th, a report arrived 13th Jan. from Colvile, saying that Omar, the sheikh of Duaim, whom we had employed as a pilot for a short time, but subsequently dismissed as incompetent, had met two men at Belal, who stated that they had accompanied a force of 1000 men from Berber to the wells of Bak, half-way between Bir Sani and El Koua; that the force was armed with rifles, and had a great quantity of ammunition, and that it was intended to attack our camp in the early morning. Cavalry patrols were at once sent out in the direction of the Berber road, and other military precautions taken. Nothing came of it; and when traced to its source, the rumour appeared to be a concoction of Omar's own, based upon the fact that two men had arrived at Belal from Bir Sani, bringing the news of a reinforcement of 50 men to El Zain, and a report of a force of 1000 men having marched from Berber, under Abdul Majid Wad el Lekalik, to reinforce the enemy at Birti.

It was, however, evident that unless something were done to stop El Zain, rumours of this sort would occur from time to time; and General Earle decided to ask Lord Wolseley's permission to make a raid upon this cluster of wells. The permission being accorded, it was decided to make the raid shortly before our advance up the river, allowing only sufficient time for the horses to have a couple of days' rest afterwards. Accordingly, on the 17th January the Egyptian Camel Regiment, with twenty camels of the Egyptian battery, carrying all the available camel water-tins, were brought from Abu Dom to Hamdab, it being given out that the water-tanks were being brought up to be overhauled by the Engineers; and orders were issued that on Sunday the 18th the General would inspect the Engineers, the Hussars, and the Camel Corps in fighting order, with two days' rations, water, &c., as if ready to march into action. Major Flood, 19th Hussars, who was to command the party, and Major Slade, of the Intelligence Department, were taken into the secret. No one else but General Earle and myself had an inkling of what was intended.

Our information was to the effect that the wells of El Koua, where great numbers of cattle and camels of the Monassir were said to be, were seven hours distant (this time would not represent more than twenty-eight miles); that the wells of Bir Sani were some two hours farther on, with the wells of Bak intervening; and that El Zain, with a party of dervishes, variously estimated at from 100 to 150, lived, with their flocks and herds, and the camels they had captured, on a hill called Jebel Katete, about two miles from Bir Sani, coming down to the wells for water.

Major Flood's instructions were to proceed with the Hussars (about 60 sabres) and Camel Corps (about 90 rifles) to the wells of El Koua, and, if possible, to Bak and Bir Sani, to surprise the Arabs, take them prisoners, burn their dwellings, and capture their camels and cattle. He was instructed to strike a blow at El Zain if possible, but not to be drawn into a serious engagement; and it was left to his judgment whether he would proceed beyond El Koua. Major Slade procured a guide, and was placed at Major Flood's disposal.

18th Jan. The parade was held on Sunday at 1 P.M. The Engineers, having been inspected, were dismissed. The mounted troops were told the General would inspect them after a short march; and they moved off into the desert, striking into a *khor* which led them by a short cut into the Berber-Dugiyet road, some five miles from Dugiyet. The secret had been well kept in camp. But it must have got out—probably through the guide, who has since joined the Mahdi—for there on the road were the unmistakable traces of the recent passage of a camel from Dugiyet in the direction of the wells. Flood marched till near midnight, and then halted about eight miles short of El Koua. He started again at 4 A.M., and reached a 19th Jan. cultivated *khor* (El Koua), where he found traces of hasty flight, but no cattle or camels. The wells gave barely sufficient water for thirty horses; the water he had with him was little more than enough for the men. The distance he had already travelled he estimated at thirty-five miles. He pushed on three miles to the end of the cultivated *khor*, where the rocks closed in and the ground became bad for cavalry; and then, considering the distance and the scarcity of water, he considered it advisable not to go farther; burned some of the Monassir huts, carried off some grain, and returned the same night to Hamdab.

The raid had not had the result hoped for; but it was sufficient to keep El Zain quiet as long as we were anywhere within striking distance of El Koua.

CHAPTER III.

HAMDAB—ORGANISATION.

The chief care of a General in the organ- <small>5th to 23d Jan.</small> isation of a force for active service is to ensure to his troops a sufficient supply of food and ammunition. This requires a sufficiency of transport, which again requires food for the transport animals. It may be assumed, as a general rule, that troops start properly clothed and armed, so that a supply of clothing and arms is only required when an expedition is likely to be prolonged.

When a General has secured for his troops the reasonable certainty of the necessary food and ammunition, he is at liberty to turn his mind to other questions of organisation, foremost in importance among which is the care of his sick and wounded, and, in all ordinary expeditions, the evacuation of the sick and wounded from his field-hospitals to hospitals upon the line of communication. It may safely be said that these questions require far more time and elaboration of detail than the strategical and tactical questions; and the system now prevailing in all European armies is to give to a General in command of an expedition a Chief of the Staff, who relieves him of this detail, and of all the minor details of camp routine, leaving the General in command free to weigh the value of the reports made by his intelligence department, and to decide by what means, strategical and tactical, he can obtain the greatest advantage over his enemy. This system ensures to the General in command time for thought, relief from small worrying cares, and leisure to mature his plans of campaign and of battle.

In the present case, the river column had some peculiar advantages in its favour,

ORGANISATION.

and some peculiar disadvantages to contend with. In the first and great matter of food for the troops, we were certain of its not failing for nearly three months. All our infantry leaving Korti brought one hundred days' food per man in their boats,—food, supposed to be of the best quality, specially prepared and packed in England. All other troops coming up in boats brought as many days' supply as they could carry, in addition to loads of material for their special services. Every effort was made to economise these supplies by obtaining cattle and native flour. Troops leaving Korti brought with them "way rations" sufficient to last to Abu Dom. There native bakers supplied them with bread baked from native flour, and fresh meat was killed for them. On arrival at Hamdab, they found a commissariat bakery, which we established immediately on arrival, by building four ovens in the river bank, each able to turn out nearly six hundred loaves a-day; and a cattle depot, which was kept supplied by local purchase. We were thus enabled to start from Hamdab with our supplies of biscuit and preserved meat almost untouched.

As originally intended in the orders given to General Earle, when he left Korti at the beginning of the year, we were to have a battalion of infantry for the special purpose of forming posts between Abu Dom and Abu Hamed, which would have greatly facilitated the forwarding of convoys of cattle after the column from Abu Dom;

15th Jan. but on the 15th, fresh orders were received to the effect that it would not be possible to give to General Earle a fifth battalion to occupy posts, that the General of communication would not establish any line of communication beyond Abu Dom, and that the river force was to be a flying column. We should therefore have to depend for food upon the supplies we could take with us from Abu Dom, upon whatever we could buy or capture in the country we were about to enter, and upon the promised convoy

ORGANISATION.

from Korosko, which was to meet us at Abu Hamed.

But we had not only to consider how to supply the European troops with food. We had to supply some 200 Egyptian troops, and 150 natives, mostly Aden camel-drivers, and to feed about 150 horses and 530 camels. The Egyptian soldiers, Camel Corps, and Artillery, agreed without a murmur to their ration being confined to 1 lb. meat and 1 lb. flour, if they were allowed a small sum, which was settled at half a piastre (about 1¼d.) daily, to supplement their ration by the purchase of vegetables or any native delicacy. The Aden camel-drivers also consented to forego their authorised ration of sugar, salt, and tea or coffee; so that we were enabled to reserve all our groceries for the European troops and Egyptian officers.

The horses—Egyptian cavalry horses—which had been handed over to the 19th Hussars at Wady Halfa, and the ponies of the staff and regimental officers, were in hard serviceable condition; but to keep them in condition, they must not be reduced below their ration of 10 lb. of grain daily, to be supplemented by such green forage as could be procured. And this meant 1500 lb. of grain daily, or five camel-loads; for we found that 300 lb. is as heavy a load as camels in good condition will, on the average, carry for several days in succession.

The Camel Corps and the Artillery had sufficient regimental transport to carry six days' rations for themselves, and six days' forage, at a daily ration of 8 lb. of grain for each camel; but all the grain for horses, all further reserve of grain for the Egyptian camels, and all the grain for the Eleventh Transport Company, had to be carried by the 350 camels of that company, which had also to carry their own European staff, with their kits, the kits of the Aden drivers, the equipment of the Hussars, certain headquarter baggage and office material, a large number of iron water-tanks—brought up in case we should be compelled to make a flanking movement to turn a position by the desert, —and all the flour for the native troops. We

ORGANISATION.

were fairly well off for transport; but we were going into an enemy's country, where no supplies were likely to be forthcoming by purchase. It was said to be a very barren country also, and we must anticipate that the small store of grain kept by the natives would be either carried off or concealed, so that it was a matter of vital importance to take the utmost possible quantity of flour and grain with us.

As it was, we were enabled to start from Hamdab, taking 24th February as the day from which the start was made, with the following supplies: about eighty-five days' boat rations for the whole European force, with the exception of sugar and salt, of which we were on very short rations throughout. The ration of sugar was reduced even before we left Hamdab from two and a half to one and a half ounces; and the ration of salt was reduced to a quarter of an ounce, and only issued on days when fresh meat was served out. This quantity of eighty-five days' supply was what was represented by the number of cases of the various kinds of food; but, before leaving Hamdab, we had become aware that in certain items, especially biscuit, preserved vegetables, rice, oatmeal, and tobacco, considerable deductions must be made for goods damaged by water, owing to defective packing, or rather defective closing of the tin cases, and to the exposure to wet to which large quantities of cases had been subject in leaky or damaged boats on the way from Sarras to Korti. We estimated the probable loss in biscuit alone at thirty per cent, almost all the "cabin biscuit" being bad; and accordingly we arranged that the convoy from Korosko was to bring to Abu Hamed supplies in the following proportions: meat, tea, lime-juice, pepper, one ration each; preserved vegetables, one and a half; biscuit, sugar, and salt, two rations each. The great loss in sugar and salt was due chiefly to their having been packed in bags, not waterproof, which had become wet; and partly, especially in sugar, to thefts by natives at the various portages along our long line of communication from Alexandria to Korti.

For the natives we started with sixty days' supply of flour, and forty days' supply of unground wheat, which could either be converted into flour, or be used for the horses, if the supply of grain should fail. We hoped to collect cattle and sheep, or to get these sent up after us, in sufficient numbers to supply the natives daily with fresh meat; and as a matter of fact, that supply did not fail us till we had reached Hebbeh, a month after our start: up to that date we were successful in supplying all the troops with fresh meat, and our preserved meat was almost untouched.

For the horses we started with nearly forty days' grain. More could not be carried for want of transport. The camels, it was evident from the first, must go short of grain, and subsist on the growing forage, unless we could obtain grain in large quantities from the country we were about to enter.

For firewood we must trust to the local supply for the day's wants: our transport would not admit of our carrying on from each bivouac more than sufficient for the following day's needs, both boats and camels being loaded up with full loads.

Such was our provision for the feeding of the troops and animals. As regards ammunition, each gun had a hundred rounds, and about 280 rounds for every rifle was carried in the boats.

Our transport was in good condition. The boats, in spite of their rough work on the way up, were serviceable. They had mostly been overhauled at Korti. Many of them bore honourable scars in the shape of tin patches, and there was rather a lack of paint, but they were fit for work. Our camels were in sound, serviceable order, and their saddles were in good condition.

The next work which demanded attention was the organisation for the care of the sick and wounded. The material for a field-hospital of 200 beds had already been forwarded to Abu Dom; but it was manifest to me, upon a cursory inspection, that it was upon a scale unsuited for our river expedition. Twenty hospital marquees were luxuries that we could not afford to carry; meat-covers and meat-skewers, however valuable elsewhere, were out of place here; large pewter measures and beer-taps still more so, in a land where no beer is. Pairs of bellows might possibly be useful, though it was doubtful; but coffee-mills could not help us, where there was no coffee. Sheets and pillows might be of great comfort, but they could only be taken in such small quantities as to be available for the worst cases; and so on through a long list, including blue waistcoats and trousers. In fact, all superfluous gear, to use the sailors' favourite word, must be abandoned—sacrificed to the stern necessity of utilising every particle of available transport for the carriage of food and ammunition.

Accordingly, I visited Korti, and there saw Surgeon-General O'Nial, the principal medical officer of the expedition, and Surgeon-Major Harvey, who was selected as senior medical officer of the river column. They met me in the fairest way. I agreed, on General Earle's part, to give them one boat for each of the eight sections of the field-hospital, and a ninth boat for the senior medical officer, in which he could take extra comforts for the sick, and to furnish a sufficient number of men to make up, with the men of the Medical Staff Corps, crews for the boats. I undertook that, if tentage was necessary, it should be provided from the tents carried by the troops in their boats. They agreed to reduce the equipment, so that each section for twenty-five patients should be carried in one boat—a few luxuries such as condensed milk, champagne, lime-juice, &c., being carried by the senior medical officer. Surgeon-Major Harvey proceeded to Abu Dom, and superintended the revision of the equipment, and its stowage in the whalers; the crews for the whalers were sent down from Hamdab. And throughout the campaign, two sections of this field-hospital accompanied each infantry battalion.

The resources of the field-hospital were made available to the utmost by the abandonment of all rules of red tape. Medical officers of corps were granted the power of admission to and discharge from the hospital, and were authorised to draw from the field-hospital at all times whatever was wanted to keep their regimental medical equipment complete.

We had no means, nor was there time at our disposal, for forming a bearer company to carry wounded out of action; but it was arranged that the eight stretchers of each battalion should accompany the battalion into action, carried by the bandsmen of the battalion. Each corps was to carry its own sick in its own boats, and the sick of mounted corps were to be carried in the boats of the battalion to which they were attached for rations. For it is one of the penalties of a flying column that it must carry forward with it, and cannot leave behind or send back, its sick and wounded.

A paymaster was sent to us with about £10,000 in money. We spent about £1500 in buying supplies, in native labour, &c., before leaving Hamdab; but from that time forward Major Mackie, our paymaster, had an easy time, for money was useless in an arid desert where there were no sellers and nothing to buy.

A veterinary surgeon accompanied the transport.

Only a few days before we left Hamdab, the telegraph was extended to an office in our fort there. This was a great boon, as it saved much time and labour hitherto expended in sending our messages to and receiving them from Abu Dom, nineteen miles away. The country was quite impracticable for heliographic signalling, owing to the absence of marked high hills, and the presence of a succession of low ridges.

Before the 24th of January a number of

ORGANISATION.

Canadian voyageurs joined the column, and were distributed among the battalions and corps in boats; and a boat-repairing party, under Lieutenant Kenney, R.E., arrived with repairing material. Its two boats' crews were from that moment almost incessantly at work.

While the work of organisation was going on, General Earle, with his own hand, drew up a series of rules for the movement of the troops in boats, for embarkations and disembarkations, for the bivouac, and for precautions on the march. He also designed special tactical formations for the march, with a view to rapidly passing from column into square, and square into column. These memoranda, together with others drawn up on the system of supply during the advance, and the medical arrangements for the troops, were circulated; and during our stay at Hamdab, the troops were frequently practised by General Earle, in the tactical formations he had devised, over the very roughest ground.

CHAPTER IV.

HAMDAB—CONCENTRATION.

5th to 23d Jan. It seemed at one time, during the earlier portion of our period of concentration at Hamdab, that the necessities of the desert column, on which so much depended, would seriously cripple us of the river route. Colonel Burnaby had been promised to us; and General Earle had hoped to have him for the command of the

6th Jan. mounted troops; but on the 6th January General Buller telegraphed, "I must steal Burnaby. I do not know who else is to

8th Jan. command Metemmeh." On the 8th General Buller still counted on sending us the West Kent Regiment, to take up posts on our

9th Jan. line of communications; but on the 9th the

first note of alarm to us was sounded.
" Every endeavour," General Buller wrote,
" will be made to complete the infantry of
your force up to 100 days' rations per man
before they start; but it is possible the
difficulties of transport may make it almost
impossible to do this within a reasonable
time. It is desirable, therefore, for you to
consider whether it may not be possible
for you to advance, say two battalions of
infantry and a portion of your artillery
and mounted men, through the Monassir
country to Abu Hamed, and so open the
line of supply from Korosko." In this
case, General Earle was to keep touch
of his rear battalions; the Mudir's troops
assisting him to do this by occupying the
Monassir country; and he was reminded
that for the present his main objective was
the capture of Berber, and that for this
purpose he must concentrate his force.

To this minute General Earle replied 10th Jan.
that he should be prepared to advance with
two battalions and the mounted troops as

soon as he had two battalions of infantry complete with 100 days' supply, together with the portion of the transport company allotted to his column, by which time he hoped to have collected forage for the animals and food for the Egyptian troops. He considered all his small force of mounted troops should accompany his advanced brigade, and he did not propose to divide them, as opposition was to be expected to that brigade in the Monassir country. He wished the Mudir's troops to march parallel to us upon the right bank, and to be ready to occupy the Monassir country as soon as he had defeated the Monassir tribe. He asked for two companies of a regiment from the line of communications to occupy Hamdab and a post in the Monassir country; and in that case anticipated no military difficulty for the troops following the leading brigade, moving in half-battalions. General Earle trusted that before he moved, his naval boat, with a Gardner gun, his boat officers and voyageurs, and boat-repairing party might have reached his camp. He urged, also, that his commissariat staff should be promptly and considerably increased.

In reply General Earle was informed, on the 15th, that most of his requests were in course of fulfilment; but that Lord Wolseley did not approve his proposal to take with him two companies of a line of communication regiment for the purpose of forming posts on his line. He was instructed that his force was to be a flying column; that the General of communications would not occupy the line behind us; and further, that it was improbable the West Kent Regiment could be rationed sufficiently in advance to enable it to follow us up the river. Our, at that time, very insufficient commissariat staff could not yet be increased, because there was no one at Korti to send to us. Our land transport was on the 14th only leaving Dongola; but Lord Wolseley was anxious that our leading battalions should advance at the very earliest moment to occupy the Monassir country, and considered it not necessary that we should wait for our transport company, desiring General Earle to advance into the Monassir country, and there await the arrival of the transport.

At this time we had not a single baggage-camel, except the few belonging to the Egyptian Camel Corps and Artillery. To attempt an advance in boats into an enemy's country by an unknown river, without cavalry to scout on the banks, would have been an act of folly; and cavalry could not move without some transport. It is true that I had moved half a troop from Korti to Hamdab without any transport animals, by carrying their forage and equipment in the boats of the Staffords, and making the horses and the boats rendezvous together at night; but that was not a manœuvre to be attempted outside a peaceful country. Indeed it is well we did not attempt it, for after the first day's advance the boats had to take a channel which effectually separated them from all touch of the horses for two days.

There was another strong reason against our immediate advance. Our leading battalion, the Staffords, had been sent up with only thirty days' supplies, of which nearly twenty were already consumed. It had to fill up from the supplies of the Duke of Cornwall's Light Infantry, which we had halted at Abu Dom, and which, in its turn, had to fill up from the West Kent. This operation could not be completed till the 22d; and if we advanced without our full quantity of supplies, we should never be able to bring them up, as our completing our required amount depended absolutely on every infantry boat taking up its full 100 days per man in the boat. How important it seemed that we should not start without our full quantity can be judged from the fact that the same post which brought the above-named instructions to General Earle, also brought him instructions that, subject to the military necessities of the situation, he was to leave at Abu Hamed a garrison of 300 men, with sixty days' supply; and at Berber a garrison of 700 men with sixty days' supply, and also 40,000 complete rations; which, with 800 *ardebs* of dourra that we were to purchase at Berber, would be required for the use of a force to be sent from Berber to Suakim.

17th Jan. General Earle, therefore, replied by telegraph to the Chief of the Staff on the 17th, that if the latter would send him forty baggage-camels, with saddles and drivers complete, at once, he could advance on the 23d, but not before, as the Staffords' supplies would not be complete sooner.

He also wrote at length, explaining the situation. He said in his memorandum: "As I am aware that there is a considerable force before us at Birti, as a prolonged halt in its immediate presence would be disadvantageous, and as I cannot inflict a severe defeat upon it without my small force of cavalry, I do not consider it advisable to advance from this camp until I can move with two battalions of infantry, the Hussars and other mounted troops, to the direct attack of the enemy's position." He repeated the arguments stated above, and his offer to advance on 23d if forty camels were sent to him, and added: "I must, however, point out, that by thus advancing without other land transport, I shall be deprived of the means of making any turning movement in the desert, which would require a day's absence of the infantry from their boats; and should difficult rapids render portaging necessary, I shall be without the means of carrying loads which the transport allotted to me was specially intended to provide."

On the 17th General Buller replied, "I have not a camel or driver to send. They are in the desert."

As regarded our power to carry out the instructions for leaving supplies at Abu Hamed and Berber, I went very carefully into calculations; and the Chief of the Staff was informed that, in the event of our starting, filled up with all the rations we could take, and receiving 50,000 rations at Korosko, we should, supposing us to be ready to leave Berber on 3d March, have at that date only twenty-eight days' supplies for the balance of our force (1800 men), after leaving the garrisons and supplies ordered at Abu Hamed and Berber. These calculations were accepted by the Chief of the Staff.

19th Jan. On the 19th, the good news reached us that our transport under Captain Lea had reached Korti, would be completed to 350 serviceable camels, and would start on the
20th Jan. 20th; and on the 20th we were told that supplies to complete all our demands would leave at once in the steamer Nassif el Kheir, with the exception of certain quantities of biscuit, sugar, cocoa and milk for hospitals, salt, soap, and tobacco. General Buller's telegram ended: "The consignment by Nassif Kheir and Lea will complete all I can send you. You must be

thankful for small mercies, and go as quickly as you can."

Colonel Butler arrived at Hamdab on the 20th, and General Earle decided to charge him with the duty of reconnoitring for the advance of the force. He was to move with the cavalry and camel corps along the bank, cover the advance of and select camping-grounds for the troops in the boats; and he was to command the advanced post whenever headquarters were not present there.[1]

Lieutenant-Colonel Alleyne with a party of voyageurs arrived on the 21st. He was charged with the direction of the advance by river, and had as his assistants Captain Orde, Rifle Brigade, Captain Lord Avonmore, Hampshire Regiment, and Lieutenant Peel, 2d Life Guards, all by this time thoroughly experienced in boat-work on the Nile.

21st Jan.

[1] At Colonel Butler's request, Major Martin, R.A., and Lieutenant Pirie, 2d Life Guards, were attached to him as staff officers.

Captain Courtney, R.E., and Captain Hon. F. Colborne, Royal Irish Rifles, arrived for the purpose of surveying the river as we advanced.

The headquarters of the 1st battalion Royal Highlanders (Black Watch) arrived in our camp on the 13th, and the battalion was completed in the course of the next few days.

21st to 23d Jan. The headquarters of the 1st battalion Gordon Highlanders arrived on the 21st, but the battalion was still incomplete on the 24th. One company had been left to garrison Halfa; and one company, with the Lieutenant-Colonel second in command, was still far behind.

The 2d battalion Duke of Cornwall's Light Infantry, after handing over its supplies to the Staffords at Abu Dom, waited there to complete its own supplies from convoys sent up from Korti. Its first half-battalion reached Hamdab on the 23d; its headquarters and remaining half on the 24th.

The camel battery marched from Abu Dom to Hamdab on the 22d, joining the camel corps there.

After placing great difficulties in the way, the Mudir of Dongola had consented to his troops advancing into the Monassir country by the right bank. I do not propose to enter into any detail of their composition, or into the story of their march. It is sufficient here to state that, after having succeeded in taking over the Vakeel's fort at Abu Dom for the use of the two companies of the Essex Regiment, which arrived there as garrison on the 23d, Colvile succeeded in getting the Mudir's troops crossed over to the right bank at Merawi on the 21st and 22d. On the 23d, to the number of 310, they made a short march out from Merawi, complete, Colvile informed us, with transport (camels and donkeys) and ammunition (120 rounds per man), but without riding-camels for scouting. They had also a brass gun, which they used to fire off at night. The

Vakeel accompanied them, saying it was necessary he should do so, to prevent ill-treatment of friendly natives. Before starting, he telegraphed to the Mudir to say that, "with God's help, he hoped to collect some taxes."

The situation in the Soudan, as known to us at this time, was as follows. Herbert Stewart, having established a post at Gakdul, had returned to Korti, had again advanced to and beyond Gakdul, and had fought the action of Abu Klea. Our knowledge of the details of that fight was very limited; but we could read between the lines of the telegrams, and could tell that Stewart had met with a very determined resistance, and that somehow the enemy had got inside the square. We were told that Stewart was continuing his advance on Metemmeh.

A messenger from Gordon, who had left for Khartoum on 18th December, had returned to Korti on 11th January; but unfortunately, on his way back his letters had been taken from him, and he had been so severely beaten he could recollect nothing. Thus our latest news from Khartoum was still the few words—"All well, 14th December," and the verbal message mentioned in the first chapter.

From Berber we had news as late as the 23d December. All was then quiet there. There were very few soldiers in the town; they were spread about in the surrounding villages—the Egyptian soldiers working as slaves at the *sakyehs*. The town was said to be surrounded by an intrenchment; and there were some guns, varying in the statements from three to six in number, on the left bank of the river at Robush or Masseed, the village opposite Berber. Mohammed el Kheir, the Mahdi's Emir of Berber, had applied to the Mahdi for reinforcements and guns, but had met with a refusal to send them.

From Abu Hamed we had news as late as the 3d January. The *sakyehs* between Berber and Abu Hamed were then at work.

Abu Hegel, chief of the Robatab, was at his own village. Sheikhs Hassan Wad Hag Said and Ali Basha were at Abu Hamed—having replaced two sheikhs who had been recalled, because they had not reported a reconnaissance to near Abu Hamed made by Major Rundle and Sheikh Saleh Bey in November.

Our latest news from Birti was of the 18th January; but we had spies there who were to inform us of any serious change in the situation. Suleiman Wad Gamr had returned from Berber, but had gone to Salamat to meet Abdul Majid Wad Abu Lekalik, who had arrived from Berber with reinforcements at least a thousand strong, and he was remaining at Salamat to bring up more reinforcements. Lekalik, as we shall hereafter call him, was on the 18th at Birti with 1500 dervishes and the Monassir and Robatab, and had been placed by the Emir of Berber in command of all the troops there. He was said to have been anxious to advance to fight us, but Sulei-

CONCENTRATION.

man had urged remaining at Birti; and now that Lekalik had agreed to remaining at Birti, Suleiman wanted to retire to the Shukook Pass. Moussa Wad Abu Hegel was still at Birti, and said to be full of fight.

To sum up the state of the information obtained through our intelligence department up to 23d January: All was well at Khartoum on 14th December; Stewart had had a hard fight, and was advancing on Metemmeh on 18th January; Berber was quiet, and not strongly defended, on 23d December; Abu Hamed had a small garrison and no defences on 3d January; a force about 3000 strong was in front of us at Birti—consisting of Berberines, Monassir, and Robatab, about 500 of them having rifles—and its commander meant fighting. Buller had told us that, from various accounts of Stewart's fight, he found that "these Arabs do charge home, and very quickly," and had advised us "not to let them get a run at us unless we were in square."

Our orders were to advance through the Monassir country, take and garrison Abu Hamed, receive a convoy from Korosko, and advance on Berber. When near Berber—within twenty miles—we were to fire a gun and two rockets every night at twelve. The desert column was to have steamers and men six or eight miles above Berber, and would answer our signal, and the steamers would then reconnoitre and assist our attack. We knew that Rundle had 700 camels ready to march from Korosko, and we had arranged signals to let him know of our proximity to Abu Hamed; and we telegraphed to Cairo asking that our letters and papers by the mail leaving Cairo 22d should be sent to Korosko to await the departure of this convoy. We also arranged for supplies of such vitally necessary material as paint for the boats and shoes for the horses being sent by the same route.

22d Jan. On the 22d Colonel Butler reconnoitred to Ooli island, and selected a site for a camp. He reported the river free from obstacles to that point. The natives had fled between Kulgeili and Ooli, but at the latter place some were remaining.

On the 23d our transport, about 330 camels, under Captain Lea, arrived at Hamdab. Arrangements were at once made for handing over regimental transport to the Hussars, the necessary transport to headquarters, and for mounting staff officers, who had been sent up to the column without any sort of mount; and then orders for the advance on the following day were issued.

23d Jan.

Colonel Hammill, of the Gordon Highlanders, was left in command at Hamdab, with orders to send on the Cornwalls by half-battalions on 25th and 26th, with two sections of the field-hospital. On the 26th he was to send on the Egyptian battery and the transport company under escort of a portion of the camel corps, left behind for this purpose, the whole under command of Major Wodehouse, R.A. He was himself to follow with his own battalion and two sections of field-hospital, as soon as his battalion was concentrated, having previously sent down to Abu Dom any superfluous stores remaining at Hamdab, and disestablished the telegraph.

General Buller, in asking me to send him a state of our force before actually starting, had said to me: "I know you have been handicapped; but now the force is completed, I mention that I know Lord Wolseley attaches great importance to your making as rapid an advance as possible;" and had asked me for the probable date of our arrival at Abu Hamed. I replied: "We start to-morrow. It is impossible to predict the date of reaching Abu Hamed. It must depend on nature of river and opposition of enemy, both unknown quantities."

CHAPTER V.

HAMDAB TO KAB EL ABD—TOUCH OF THE ENEMY.

BEFORE General Earle left Korti, Lord Wolseley gave him some dates of probable moves, which he entered in his pocket-book. The first of these was, " Leave Hamdab, 24th January." We were punctual to our time. On the morning of the 24th the advance commenced at 7 A.M. The Hussars and half the camel corps marched at seven, their baggage and head-quarter baggage following at 10 o'clock under an escort of mounted troops. Two companies of the Staffordshire, with Lieut.-Colonel Alleyne and the other boat officers, moved off by river at seven, followed by

_{24th Jan.}

the boats of the Royal Engineers, and then the remainder of the battalion. The Black Watch followed at eight; the boat-repairing party, the senior medical officer, half the field-hospital, two headquarter boats, and three guard boats manned by Gordon Highlanders, moving between the half-battalions of the Black Watch. The masts of all whalers were lowered before starting, as we were about to commence a long journey against the prevailing north wind.

Headquarters marched about 11 A.M. Before starting we telegraphed to Korti: "Just off; all going as well as possible; troops in high spirits, longing for a fight; no sick." As we rode along the bank we saw many boats in difficulties. The channel was full of sunken rocks; and nine boats had to be unloaded, hauled up, and repaired either by their own crews or the boat-repairing party. The last boats did not arrive opposite Ooli island, about eight miles from Hamdab, till 7 P.M.; but by half-past 7 we were all in bivouac. The anchorage on the left bank being scanty, the Black Watch bivouacked on the right bank opposite. The position for the bivouac of the Staffords and mounted troops was on a high Nile island—that is to say, on land which, though now connected with the mainland, would at high Nile be entirely separated from it by a wide deep channel, now only partially full and crossed by a causeway.

On the arrival of the leading boats, the mounted troops reconnoitred along the left bank, a short distance beyond Kabour, and found the country deserted. Two of the boat officers reconnoitred by river. The result of the combined reports, and of native information, was that the channel along the left bank was impracticable for boats; and it was decided that the channel on the right bank, on the far side of Great Ooli island, must be used. It was found that it could be reached from the left bank channel by a narrow dyke between Great Ooli island and another small island just opposite the camp of the Staffords.

And now commenced our first military difficulty, necessitating the first of those moves in the game of chess which we subsequently had to play. The infantry was about to be effectually separated from the mounted troops. Any boats sent into the rapids in the right-bank channel would be as completely separated from us for the time being as if they were a hundred miles away. A force of 3000 of the enemy was known to be within eighteen miles of us; and in the rocky and difficult country into which we had now entered, every move must be made with caution. If there was one thing more important than another, it was that we should avoid the smallest chance of being surprised. It would not do to send a small force of 60 Hussars and 40 Egyptian Camel Corps to bivouac by themselves in advance on the left bank. Yet the head of the rapid through which the troops were about to pass must be held, and cavalry must scout well to its front. It was therefore decided to march half a battalion of the Black Watch to the neighbourhood of Kabour to form a post there, with the cavalry and camel corps at a point where the Staffords, who were to be sent into the right-bank channel, would again emerge into the main stream at the head of Suffi island.

About 7 P.M. we got into heliographic communication with Colvile, who had, with the Mudir's troops, reached Ummerikh, on the right bank opposite our bivouac. We sent over a signaller to relieve one of his who had been touched by the sun, and at the same time ordered him to advance the following day on the right bank to the head of the rapid (known as Edermih cataract) into which we were about to launch the Staffords.

Information as to the channel between Hamdab and our present bivouac was sent back to Hamdab, for the use of the troops who were to follow, and the messenger took back our report of progress for the Chief of the Staff.

On the morning of the 25th, Colonel

25th Jan. Butler moved off with the mounted troops, and selected a strong position for the advanced post on a small rocky high Nile island, just above the head of Suffi island; and the half-battalion Black Watch arrived there at 10 o'clock. The Staffords had moved into the dike leading to the right-bank channel at 6.45 A.M., and soon after 8 o'clock their last boat was lost to view. Half the battalion Black Watch remained at Ooli bivouac, where, in the course of the day, they were joined by the leading half-battalion of the Duke of Cornwall's Light Infantry.

General Earle with his staff rode to the advanced post, arriving there about 11 A.M. Communication by heliograph was at once established with the Ooli bivouac, and about the same time the Mudir's troops arrived at Mushra el Abiad on the opposite bank, and Colvile established his heliograph there.

We then rode up the river as far as Kabenat, about three miles beyond Kabour. Here we found a strong fort, with walls eight to twelve feet thick built of loose stones, and capable of holding a garrison of 500 men, on the top of a high detached hill, completely commanding the river and bank; and a similar fort opposite on the right bank, with swift and difficult water flowing between. Who built these forts? From what period do they date? There is a vague tradition among the Soudanese that they were built by some Christian power some centuries ago, and I am satisfied these forts are of comparatively modern date. Ascending to the fort, we obtained an extended view, and were shortly joined by Colonel Butler, who told us he had reconnoitred to the cataract of Kab el Abd, five miles further on. He reported the country clear and fairly open, and the water fairly clear up to Kab el Abd, the cataract there being like the big gate of Semneh. All the country beyond Ooli camp was deserted.

We returned to Kabour post, and about 4 P.M. got into communication by heliograph with Colonel Alleyne on Suffi island. He told us three complete companies were through the cataract; so he was ordered to send on two companies to relieve the half-battalion Black Watch, which Colonel Butler was ordered to send back to Ooli as soon as relieved. Colvile was directed to keep the Mudir's troops halted till further orders. Instructions were sent back to Hamdab to detain the artillery and transport there till further orders, and to send two officers of the Gordon Highlanders to view the river as far as Kabenat, in order to expedite the advance of the battalion later on. General Earle and staff then returned to the Ooli bivouac.

Two companies of the Staffords reached the Kabour advanced post shortly after dark; but as the pickets of the Black Watch were posted, Colonel Butler did not relieve them, and the half-battalion did not return to Ooli till the following morning.

26th Jan. At the usual hour on the 26th (6.45 A.M.), the half-battalion Black Watch at Ooli, with one boat of repairing party, and field-hospital, moved off into the Edermih cataract, piloted by a boat officer sent back for the purpose, and followed by the second half-battalion, as soon as it arrived from Kabour. The second half-battalion of the Cornwalls arrived at Ooli.

General Earle and his staff again rode to Kabour. The Staffords completed the passage of the cataract, and concentrated at the advanced post. In the afternoon we embarked in a whaler and crossed to the Mudir's camp, where General Earle inspected the Mudir's troops under Achmet Effendi. The Vakeel was living in a tent, with carpets and cushions—a great contrast to our primitive open-air bivouac. Coffee was served, the situation was discussed, and we then dropped down in our boat to the head of Suffi island, where we met Colonel Alleyne, and walked with him to the cataract. The leading wing of the Black Watch was passing through, and the rear wing was closing up at the foot of the rapid. The cataract (Edermih) was a very troublesome one. In the first place, two small shoots or rapids had to be tracked up; then came three-quarters of a mile of swift broken rapids, with four shoots or rushes of water, the last of which was like the great gate of Semneh. Arms, ammunition, and accoutrements had to be portaged for three-quarters of a mile, and the crews of three boats had to be employed to haul one boat through. Alleyne thought it was as bad water as any on the river.

We returned to Kabour, and thence to Ooli, leaving orders with Colonel Butler to advance with the Staffords and as many of the Black Watch as possible to Kab el Abd next day. Only two companies of the Black Watch reached Kabour that night.

Orders were sent to Colonel Hammill at Hamdab for the artillery and transport to march with their escort on the 28th. Colvile was instructed to move in the morning with the Mudir's troops, and take up a position opposite Kab el Abd. Meanwhile he was to urge the Vakeel to keep his troops in hand, as they had been setting fire to huts, and we were in a theoretically friendly country. The Cornwalls were ordered to advance into the Edermih cataract in the morning.

In the night one of our spies returned from Birti. He brought word that on Saturday the 24th there were at Birti some 2500 men, under five chiefs, of whom the most prominent were Lekalik, Suleiman Wad Gamr, and Moussa Wad Abu Hegel. He told us it was their intention to attack us when our boats were separated in the cataract of Kab el Abd, or beyond it, and that they meant to attack in the early morning, when it was cold.

Colonel Butler was then further instructed to push on to the foot of Kab el Abd, and concentrate the two leading battalions there. He was to reconnoitre with the mounted troops till he should get touch of the enemy, endeavouring to ascertain his strength and position, and falling back upon the infantry; and Colvile was directed to advance his troops only as far as Shebabit, and to push a reconnaissance on the right bank as nearly opposite to Birti as he could reach, endeavouring to ascertain the enemy's strength and position there.

27th Jan. On the 27th the Cornwalls advanced into the Edermih cataract, and the Staffords and Black Watch concentrated about a mile short of Kab el Abd cataract, where headquarters joined them. A strong position was taken up here, and a zareeba made. It was ascertained that the great gate of the cataract could be avoided by tracking up the opposite bank.

Meanwhile the mounted troops advanced, and some two and a half miles beyond the cataract sighted about 120 of the enemy on foot, with seven or eight horsemen, near the tomb of a sheikh at Warag. Shots were exchanged at about a thousand yards, and the enemy retiring, a further advance was made. Colonel Butler reported on return to camp that about two miles above the great gate of Kab el Abd there commenced two miles of bad rapid water.

The news of the river was bad. We seemed to have entered upon a succession of troublesome rapids. The land, too, was as bad as it could well be—nothing but black rocks and sand everywhere; scarcely a scrap of cultivation visible. But the news that the cavalry had really exchanged shots with the enemy cheered us, and there were tangible results in the shape of four camels, six oxen, and sixty sheep, captured by Marriott's camel corps. General Earle, telegraphing that night, reported, "Troops in excellent spirits, and only seven slight cases of sickness in whole force."

Meanwhile Colvile had not let the grass grow under his feet. No sooner had he reached Shebabit than, mounting ten of the Mudir's men on ten of his best baggage-camels, he pushed on with them fourteen miles to Hush el Jeruf, the village right opposite Birti, whence he obtained a good view of the enemy's camp. He described it to us as situated on a gentle slope, running down from a low range of hills to the river, the ground being broken and rocky, and the camp commanded on all sides. Owing to the nature of the ground it was difficult to see distinctly, but his impression was that there were not more than 1000 of the enemy. Three tents were visible. About 300 of the enemy had collected on a rise in the ground, and watched his party.

On his return over a succession of what at high Nile would be islands, but which had now a dry channel between them and the mainland, he met with no opposition, but was followed by a small body of horse and foot. He learned that several desertions had taken place from among the enemy.

He described the population on the right bank as remaining at work on its *sakyehs*, and presenting, therefore, a very different appearance to that of the barren deserted waste through which we were passing on the left bank.

That evening we received through Korti a long telegram from Colonel Rundle at

Korosko, giving details of the tribes who, according to the report of his sheikhs, were gathered to oppose us at Birti. It wound up thus : " I can get none of the sheikhs to go below 10,000 as the force in front of General Earle. They have no doubt now of their intention to fight."

Orders were issued for the advance to commence at the usual hour in the morning ; and Colvile was directed to cover the advance of the boats on the right bank, and endeavour to communicate with our signallers on Mishami ridge.

CHAPTER VI.

KAB EL ABD TO GAMRA—RETREAT OF THE ENEMY.

28th Jan.   EARLY on the 28th the infantry advanced in their boats. The Staffords and Black Watch passed through the Kab el Abd cataract, with damage to two boats of the Black Watch, and reached a point in the rapids about two miles distant from their camp of the previous night, immediately opposite the foot of Kandi island. The anchorage on the left bank was apparently insufficient for two battalions, and the Black Watch bivouacked on Kandi island—the Staffords occupying a semicircular position, which was covered by a zareeba, with outposts and sentries placed on a bastion-like hill in front of the camp. It was a most unsatisfactory military position; but we were on this occasion, as on others, compelled to bivouac on sites badly suited for defence, as we were restricted in the choice of sites by the limit of distance the boats could travel, and the necessity for bivouacking where there was anchorage. This was a wind-swept, sun-baked, dusty spot, without shade by day or shelter by night, at the extremity of a ridge of forbidding black rocks known as Mishami ridge.

Meanwhile the Cornwalls completed the passage of the Edermih cataract, begun on the previous day, and reached the foot of Kab el Abd, where we had bivouacked the previous night.

Our mounted troops reconnoitred as far as Rahami cataract, seven or eight miles to the front; and Colonel Butler reported no signs of the enemy. It would, he considered, be possible to push a battalion through the rapids immediately in front of us by nightfall on the 29th, but it would be necessary to portage arms and ammunition.

Colvile had vainly tried to find a position on the right bank opposite us; but the rocky nature of the ground, and the numerous islands intervening between the right and left bank, made it impossible. He, however, found a safe camping-ground on Umkumtata island nearly opposite Gamra, about three miles above our camp at Mishami ridge, all the channels between the islands themselves, and between the islands and the right bank, being sufficiently dry to admit of their being crossed by the Mudir's troops.

Our artillery and transport, with an escort of half Major Marriott's Egyptian Camel Corps, marched from Hamdab, and took up a position, surrounded by a zareeba, on some open ground about a mile in our rear, where there was a certain amount of forage and a good watering-place for the camels.

29th Jan. At 6.45 on the 29th, six companies of the Black Watch marched to Warag, and took up a position on fairly open ground at the head of the rapid; while the mounted troops pushed on, with orders from General Earle that they were to push home to Birti and bring back information as to the enemy's strength. The Cornwalls passed through the Kab el Abd cataract, and arrived at Mishami ridge, when we at once proceeded to form a zareeba on a horse-shoe-topped hill, which we held at night with the Cornwalls and half the Black Watch.

The Staffords entered the Umhaboah rapid at the same early hour. It proved to be the worst piece of water yet encountered, and it was with great difficulty and labour that four companies succeeded in working their way to Warag by sunset. Meanwhile the Black Watch had been forming a zareeba; and as soon as the half-battalion of the Staffords reached it, two companies of the Black Watch marched back to Mishami ridge, leaving half a battalion at Warag with the Staffords. The other wing of the Staffords bivouacked together in a zareeba about half-way through the rapid.

In the course of the morning a report was received from Colonel Colvile that a spy had returned from Birti with news that reinforcements from Berber, which would bring the Birti force up to 5000 men, had left Salamat on the 27th, and were to reach Birti on the 29th. Part of this force was said to be advancing on the right bank; and as General Earle did not wish Colonel Colvile and the Mudir's troops to run any risk of being attacked by superior force in an isolated position, he directed Colvile to fall back to the end of Kandi island, opposite Mishami ridge. Colvile came himself with a few men, and was brought over to our camp in a boat; but the Vakeel protested against falling back, as it would tire his men, and he could not find anywhere on the islands so good and open a position as the one he was in. As the Mudir's troops seemed to be free from anxiety as to their position, General Earle did not press his order for their return.

Orders were sent back to Hamdab directing the Gordon Highlanders to move without fail on the 30th; and a boat officer who had been twice through Edermih cataract and once through Kab el Abd, was sent to pilot them from Ooli.

On Colonel Butler's return at night, we learnt the result of his reconnaissance. He had pushed to within a mile of Birti, and had found the hills approaching close to the river, leaving only a narrow space for the road, which was rough, stony, and broken. He had come in sight of a body of the enemy about 700 to 800 yards distant, apparently advancing, and had retired from the broken ground, and taken up a position. Slade had ascended a hill from which he had looked down on the enemy's camp, and had seen a body of them, whose number he estimated at 2000, parading with the apparent object of advancing. Marriott on the right had fallen in with a scouting-party of the enemy, and had exchanged shots, having one camel killed. He had worked down a wady to the right, from which he had seen three camps of the enemy.

News reached us to-day that Herbert Stewart had advanced on the 18th, and had had a second fight on the 19th. We were told that the enemy did not charge home so well as on the 17th, and that our men's steady volleys had been too much for them; but that they shot well with their Remingtons. Our troops, we learnt, were strongly intrenched at Goubat, two miles south of Metemmeh, which was still held by the enemy. Four of Gordon's steamers were co-operating with us, of which two had started on the 24th for Khartoum with Sir C. Wilson and a small detachment of the Sussex Regiment. Herbert Stewart, we were told, was severely wounded, but was progressing satisfactorily, and great hopes were entertained of his recovery. Talbot with a large convoy had reached Gakdul from Goubat. Half the Royal Irish had left Korti on the 28th; the remainder and West Kent were to follow. Wilson reported large reinforcements marching from Berber to Metemmeh. General Buller was going to take command, and told us that "if Khartoum is sufficiently provisioned, we don't mean to do anything until you join us."

Our situation was aggravating. The desert column already on the Nile above Metemmeh, and proposing to wait there till we could join them; the enemy in force in our front ten miles away; and our troops scattered along these terrible rapids, which seemed to grow more and more difficult with each mile of our advance. There was nothing for it but to push on, and concentrate a sufficient force within striking distance of the enemy, who was apparently resolved to hold his ground at Birti.

I for one slept lightly that night. It was bitterly cold, and there was no escaping the wind. A full moon, which we hoped was to light us to victory at Birti, was shining. More than once I walked round the zareeba, where our sentries were standing motionless, looking out over the rocks and ravines around. At last I was sleeping soundly, when I was awakened by the field-officer of the Black Watch on duty, who told me that a native dressed in white had crept up, leading a horse, to within a few yards of the zareeba, had looked down upon our cavalry below, and had then made off again. Did it portend an early attack? If so, we were ready at any moment. The first note of alarm by one of our sentries would have brought all our men, armed and accoutred, to their feet, and have lined the zareeba with a circle of bayonets, and of rifles ready to sweep the surrounding space with their fire. Should we hear firing from either of our smaller advanced posts, and have to march to their assistance; or was it only a bold spy, come to learn our strength and dispositions for defence?

Nothing came to disturb us further.
30th Jan. *Réveillé* sounded at five; and the troops stood to their arms as usual. Our cavalry patrols went out, and to them at once

surrendered himself the gentleman who had visited us the night before. His story was as follows : He had been an Egyptian soldier, one of the garrison of Berber, when that place was taken by the Mahdi; he had been made to join the Mahdi's troops; he had been one of the force which marched from Berber to Birti under Lekalik, and had been made to take command of a body of riflemen there, commanding outposts at night, and visiting the troops by day. He said that on the previous night he had deserted, bringing with him a horse, the property of Moussa Wad Abu Hegel, and his rifle and ammunition. He told us that the force at Birti consisted of 5000 Monassir, 4000 Robatab, and 6000 Bisharin and Berberines; but that there were only 300 rifles, and thirty rounds of ammunition per rifle. He said that the gun from Stewart's steamer was there, but spiked and without ammunition. Lekalik had first seen our scouts on the 25th; he had then intended occupying Mishami ridge, but found it held by us on the 28th. The enemy had made a stone parapet, facing the road and river at Birti, but no other defences; and they intended standing there, though the Robatab were deserting. Lekalik and Moussa had followed our retiring scouts yesterday on horseback; and drums were beating all evening. Our friend told us that Lekalik had received a letter from Berber telling him there had been a great fight at Metemmeh.

There was nothing in this information to alter the dispositions made for the day. Half a battalion of the Cornwalls marched to Warag, and relieved the wing of the Black Watch there. The Staffords continued their advance through the cataract, and concentrated at Warag, where also half a battalion of the Black Watch arrived in its boats. The other wing of the Black Watch, after its return to Mishami, entered the Umhaboah cataract, but did not get through, bivouacking where half the Staffords had bivouacked on the previous

RETREAT OF THE ENEMY. 99

night. The Cornwalls remained at Mishami ridge. Headquarters and the mounted troops moved to Warag. Cavalry had a quiet day, vedettes out, and nothing of importance occurred.

Above Warag there still lay two miles of bad rapid water to Gamra, where there was excellent anchorage and camping-ground. Gamra was about seven miles from Birti, and General Earle decided to concentrate three battalions, the mounted troops, and artillery there; and to make it the point from which he would march to attack the enemy, leaving his boats and transport covered by a strong detachment in a good zareeba, with clear field of fire. Accordingly on the 31st he marched the Staffords by 31st Jan. land to Gamra, covered by the mounted troops. On arrival they prepared the ground, and made a zareeba for the Black Watch, who advanced in boats, being so much retarded by the difficult water that they did not succeed in concentrating at Gamra till 7 P.M., when the Staffords marched back to Warag. The Cornwalls, in the meantime, entered the Umhaboah cataract; six companies reached Warag, and two bivouacked in rear. Their reserve ammunition was carried on camels to Gamra.

Colonel Butler's report of the direct road along the river to the enemy's camp did not seem to favour a direct attack. We should apparently have to force our way through a gorge between rocks and river, commanded by hills on our right; and should, on emerging, find ourselves faced by the enemy's stone parapet, of which the deserter had told us. It was therefore very desirable, from tactical as well as strategical reasons, to find a way by which we could outflank the position; and I was sent by General Earle to ascertain if such a way was to be found. Accompanied by Colonel Butler, Colonel Colvile, Major Slade, and the deserter from Birti, I reconnoitred with the mounted troops to the south-east into the desert; and ascending a high detached hill about six miles from our camp, and four and a half miles from Birti, discovered that the low hills which enclosed the position of Birti formed a semicircle, with its flanks on the river; that immediately behind the hills there ran, straight from the hill on which we were, a broad *khor* or wady,—a dry sandy watercourse, which struck the river beyond the enemy's camp, and at the end of which we could see the palm-trees on the river-bank that marked —so our deserter said—the site of Suleiman Wad Gamr's abode. It was evident that from this wady there were branches leading straight into the enemy's camp, and the deserter assured us it was so. Here then was our line of attack clearly marked out, and the more satisfactorily that the *khor* could be reached from the camp at Gamra without passing over more than about two miles of broken ground.

It struck us at the time as singular that we saw no signs of the enemy's presence, —not a man on the look-out, not a beast grazing on the shrubs and coarse grass of the wady; and I should have pushed our reconnaissance along the wady, were it not that, feeling sure General Earle would adopt this line of attack, I did not like to show our hand. Up to this time the enemy evidently considered us only capable of moving along the river-bank, and it would be dangerous to disabuse their minds too soon.

On our return to camp in the evening, Slade proceeded to examine at length a deserter who had come into our camp in the morning, but whom he had only cursorily questioned before our start to reconnoitre. From this man he learnt that on the previous day—a report having been received at Birti that the English would attack from the desert side, and that the Turks (Mudir's troops) would advance on the right bank—a council of war had been held, at which it was decided to retire. The troops had broken up at sunset, and marched (about 1500 in number) towards Salamat, with the intention, this deserter said, of going to the Shukook pass. So, if this were true, Birti was empty at the very time we were reconnoitring for the best way to attack it.

Before starting with me in the morning, Colvile had received a letter from the Vakeel. I must preface what is coming by saying that the Vakeel, when at Korti at New Year, had been promised a very handsome reward if he were instrumental in catching Suleiman Wad Gamr and the blind man, and was very eager to earn it. His letter now was to the effect that last night (30th), Omar, Suleiman's uncle, had come in, and asked the Vakeel to promise him for the remainder of his tribe and Suleiman, that nobody would hurt them. The Vakeel had promised that no harm should happen to them or to Suleiman, whereupon Omar had gone back to bring them. "We shall get them by these means," said the Vakeel, "and then we can do what we like." The Vakeel was in high spirits over this joyful news, which must have been rather damped by Colonel

Colvile's reply: "We will treat Omar and his brothers well if they come in; but the only promise we can make to Suleiman Wad Gamr and Colonel Stewart's murderers is, that we will hang them if we catch them."

Colvile, as soon as he returned to our camp, crossed over and saw the Vakeel, reminded him of his repeated instructions to make no terms with Suleiman Wad Gamr, and said his proposal could not be for a moment entertained. To this he replied that the only way we could get through our difficulties was by leading Suleiman to believe we were his friends, and killing him afterwards. On Colvile refusing to listen to such a proposal, the Vakeel handed him a letter of remonstrance, saying that if we could bring in Suleiman, the tribes before us would be scattered; if not, we should have great trouble. Colvile then returned to our camp, and in the course of the evening received another letter from the Vakeel, saying that Omar and Abu Bekr, Suleiman's uncles, had come into his camp as friends, asserting that they had sent Lekalik and Moussa, with their people, away out of their country, and that they held their own people to be with the Government. This was rather amusing, considering that neither Omar nor Abu Bekr had any authority over the Monassir, and that Lekalik and Moussa had only retired the night before to seek a better position in the Shukook pass.

Colvile was directed to inform the Vakeel immediately that General Earle distinctly refused to acknowledge, and repudiated, any promises made to Suleiman Wad Gamr; and that General Earle had been sent here to punish Suleiman and the other murderers of Colonel Stewart and the English and French Consuls, and to punish those who had made themselves accomplices in the murder by not bringing in Suleiman as a prisoner. Colvile was further instructed to proceed at an early hour on the 1st to the Vakeel's camp, and bring him over to see General Earle, bringing over at the same time Omar and Abu Bekr.

Colonel Butler was directed to reconnoitre to Birti with the mounted troops as early as possible in the morning of the 1st; half a battalion of the Black Watch was directed to march towards Birti in support of his reconnaissance; and all troops in rear of Gamra were ordered to advance by boat.

CHAPTER VII.

BIRTI—HALT, AND ADVANCE OF THE ENEMY.

At the usual early hour on the 1st February, 1st Feb. the troops moved as ordered. Colonel Butler entered Birti, and found it deserted; his scouts, pushing three miles farther, found traces of the enemy's retreat. As soon as his report arrived, the wing of the Black Watch, which had been pushed on in support, was ordered back; and as the leading Staffords arrived at Gamra, the other wing of the Black Watch was pushed on into the Rahami cataract, and a wing of the Cornwalls was ordered on into the rapids to follow the Staffords. The artillery and convoy were ordered up from their position in rear of Mishami to Gamra.

Colonel Colvile brought over the Vakeel into our camp. Gaudet seemed incapable of believing we were so stupid as to be in earnest in refusing to capture Suleiman by promises of safety, with a view to putting him to death subsequently; but at last our dull obstinacy overcame him, and he believed. He still, however, had some hopes of catching Suleiman through the agency of Omar and Abu Bekr, and accordingly they were allowed to return to his camp, where Colvile also returned. Later in the day, however, he learned that Suleiman had fled beyond recall. He then threw up his hand in disgust, and withdrew his opposition to our issuing the proclamation offering rewards for the apprehension of Suleiman and the blind man, which he had hitherto declared would remove the last hope of capturing either of them.

His interview with the Vakeel ended, General Earle rode on to the advanced post of the Black Watch, and as soon as he received Colonel Butler's report that

Birti was deserted, he rode on there. He discovered the boat of Colonel Stewart's steamer on the shore, and there came running to him a man who announced himself to be Hassain, the stoker of the ill-fated steamer. Hassain gave the story of the wreck and the murder in detail. It differed little from the accounts so well known, and so often published; but it fixed the date of the murder as Thursday, 18th September, and it more directly connected Suleiman with the murder than any account we had yet heard. He had made his way down the river after the murder, had been taken prisoner, and kept safe by Omar, Suleiman's uncle, who had used him as a slave. We were anxious to keep him with us, that he might identify the site of the murder on our reaching Hebbeh; but he was eager to return to his home in Upper Egypt, and soon made his escape.

Our mounted troops fell back to Gamra, and that night we bivouacked as under :—

Half the Black Watch in advance of Gamra in the Rahami cataract.

Headquarters, mounted troops, Staffords, half the Black Watch, artillery, and convoy at Gamra.

Half the Cornwalls at Warag, and half in the Umhaboah cataract between Warag and Mishami.

The Gordons were through the Edermih cataract; and Captain Orde, the boat officer sent to pilot them, reported that cataract far worse than when he had passed it before, owing to the considerable fall of the river.

In reading through the rough diary of our daily proceedings, I am struck by the frequency of the expression applied to the rapids: "The worst yet encountered," or "the most difficult yet met with." The fact is, that from Ooli to Birti the river was but a succession of rapids as bad as it was possible for the boats to pass. If there was one part worse than another, it was the series of rapids along the left bank between Gamra and Birti, known as the Rahami cataract. Into this half the Black Watch had already penetrated; and the remaining wing was sent forward early on the 2d February.

2d Feb.

All our boat officers were suffering in health from constant exposure to the sun, severe physical fatigue, and the incessant strain upon their energies. There was danger of their breaking down; and accordingly, two additional officers were selected and appointed to act as boat officers —Lieutenant Morris, D.C.L.I., and Lieutenant Livingstone of the Black Watch. The rapids immediately before us proved fully sufficient to tax their powers to the utmost.

General Earle considered it important to occupy Birti at once; and as the news of the enemy's movements justified him in pushing forward the mounted troops alone, Colonel Butler was sent on with the Hussars and camel corps to form a zareeba and hold it. Having formed a zareeba, he reconnoitred five miles in advance, and came upon some baggage and provisions abandoned by the enemy. He saw no inhabitants. The river was smooth, resembling a Scotch loch; the country along the shore exceedingly rough, with rocks coming down to near the river.

A refugee from the rebel camp reported that the rebels had halted a day at the entrance to the Shukook pass, but when they heard that the English were in Birti they had retired farther. He had heard that Lekalik and Suleiman were going to Berber, and Moussa to the Robatab country. There had been many desertions since Birti was abandoned, and Suleiman, who had seen the proclamation offering a reward for his capture, was reported to be in great alarm. A report from Colonel Colvile, however, said that the information brought to the Vakeel was to the effect that the rebels were halted, and were holding the Shukook pass.

The leading wing of the Black Watch

was, early in the day, engaged in overcoming a most serious succession of bad rushes of water; and its progress was very slow. Alleyne resolved to try, if possible, to find another passage, and sent Colonel Denison, with his crew of voyageurs, to examine another channel on the north of the great island opposite us. I rode on to Birti, and there found Colonel Denison, who had succeeded in passing through this northern channel, and reported it, though difficult, by no means so bad as the southern channel. Accordingly, on my return, all troops not already committed to the left bank were diverted into this channel; but seven companies of the Black Watch had advanced too far to return with safety. The troops worked till dusk, and then bivouacked by half-battalions on the high bank above their boats in the Rahami cataract. The Cornwalls, with headquarters, artillery, and convoy, bivouacked at Gamra.

On the following day (3d) the Cornwalls entered the cataract; and headquarters, 3d Feb.

with the artillery and convoy, marched to Birti, where, late in the evening, five companies of the Staffords arrived by the northern passage after twelve hours' unremitting toil. The whole of the remainder of the infantry was still struggling through the cataract; but the General had not hesitated to push forward the convoy, there being no fear of attack, and the ground at Birti offering an admirable site for an encampment, and ample supplies of growing forage.

The Mudir's troops occupied the village of Hush el Jeruf on the right bank opposite our camp, and Colvile reported that his information was that the rebels had retired beyond the Shukook pass, that no resistance was to be expected there, that Suleiman's movements were uncertain, and that it was doubtful whether he had or had not fled to Berber. One of our own spies, however, brought us in apparently more definite information. He said that Lekalik and Moussa were encamped at the far end of the Shukook pass; that they had given

Suleiman six days to collect his cattle and family at Salamat, promising to hold the pass for that time, but no longer; and that then Suleiman was to go with Lekalik across the desert to Abu Egli, Moussa returning to his own country.

The mounted troops patrolled some six miles to the front; and Colonel Butler reported that he had found a site for a camp about this distance forward, which was equally suitable for one battalion or for two, with forage and good ground for mounted troops, and that there was nothing but clear water between it and Birti. The General therefore decided to push forward the mounted troops and the Staffords on the following day.

Meanwhile the houses in Birti had been carefully searched by our intelligence officers, and large quantities of papers found were examined. Some few relics of Stewart's party were discovered, fragments of French and English books, a portion of an English "field boot," the broken face and case of an aneroid barometer, which I have since ascertained was sold to Stewart an hour or two before his departure from Charing Cross with General Gordon. These were all found in Suleiman Wad Gamr's house. Every effort was made to ascertain correctly which houses, trees, and *sakyehs* were the property of Suleiman Wad Gamr, and of any prominent rebels; and a list of them was prepared.

For the first time since leaving Belal we found ourselves in a well-cultivated country. Birti was an oasis in the wilderness of hideous rocks, through which for ten days we had been wending our weary way. Both on the mainland and on the high hill island opposite there were many *sakyehs*, and plentiful green crops. Our commissariat officers, with the camels of the transport company, were engaged in searching for grain. Some was found in the houses, and much more buried in pits on the island.

The enemy's camp had been situated

on uncultivated ground, some distance below (down-stream of) the village of Birti itself. A semicircle of low rocky hills surrounded it, the ends of the semicircle resting on the river. In the midst of it there was a low rocky eminence; and on this, on the slopes of the hills, and on the flat ground below, the dervishes had constructed their shelters of boughs of trees and straw mats. One of the most curious features of the camp was the number of places of prayer of large size, prepared on spaces of flat ground by clearing away all stones, carefully marked out by lines of stones, with the same point towards the east, with which we are all familiar on oriental prayer-carpets. Judging by my experience of native camps built in a similar way in Ashanti, I should say there had been from 1500 to 2000 men encamped here. We could see where the tents of the three chiefs had been, and the stables of their horses. Nothing of any value was found in the camp: a few cooking-pots, walking-sticks, one or two pieces of wood with verses from the Koran written on them, some inferior straw mats, were all that we could find. No arms of any kind were discovered; but a thousand rounds of Remington ammunition were found in one of the houses. The broad wady by which we had purposed to march to the attack led directly round the back of the camp to the cultivated ground behind, and had wide easy passages leading right into the heart of the camp. It was a matter of sore regret to us not to have found the enemy here; and it became evident to us that unless they deliberately stayed to meet us, we never could hope to overtake them. Already the head of the Black Watch had been three days in the Rahami cataract, and not a boat had reached Birti.

4th Feb. On the morning of the 4th, the Staffords closed up at Birti, and six companies were sent on by river, their advance covered by the mounted troops. The leading companies arrived at the site selected by

Colonel Butler, and by him christened Castle Camp, at noon. Butler reconnoitred along the bank for between three and four miles farther over exceedingly broken ground, where horses had frequently to be led in single file. A mile and a half above Castle Camp the rapids began again; but Alleyne, who reconnoitred in his boat to their foot, and examined them, pronounced that they could be passed. A mile above Castle Camp, a large island (Dulka) began, and extended from three to four miles. On the opposite side of the island there appeared to be a stretch of clear water; but Alleyne, who examined it, discovered much broken water and many islands beyond.

During the day the Black Watch concentrated at Birti. They had been four days in the cataract, seven miles in length, working from dawn to dusk. They had lost one man drowned, and two boats. The last two companies of the Staffords were also kept at Birti, five of their boats being in need of repair. They were all ordered to advance to Castle Camp on the 5th; but no orders were issued for any advance beyond that place, pending Colonel Butler's reconnaissance report, which did not arrive till the following day.

A party of Royal Engineers and two companies of the Black Watch, under instructions of the intelligence officers, were employed in destroying Suleiman Wad Gamr's houses, date-palms, and *sakyehs*.

The Cornwalls were still in Rahami cataract, and news arrived that the Gordons had passed through Kab el Abd cataract. A boat officer was sent back from Birti to pilot them on, and to relieve the one who had brought them through Edermih and Kab el Abd.

General Earle hoped now to be able to move the Cornwalls forward from Birti on the 6th; and he therefore gave orders to Colonel Colvile to instruct the Vakeel to cross the Mudir's troops over on the 6th to the left bank, with a view to their remaining in occupation of the Monassir country during our advance to Berber.

The General also, thinking that the Vakeel could be of great use to him in his advance as far as Salamat by collecting information, directed Colvile to request him to cross over with an escort on the 5th, in readiness to advance with our headquarters on the 6th. Colvile was himself to come over, and to bring with him Suleiman's uncles and some other sheikhs who had surrendered to the Vakeel. This was in compliance with Lord Wolseley's orders that we were to take on to Berber all sheikhs who might come into our camp, as hostages for the good behaviour of their people in our rear.

Colvile heliographed back that the Vakeel did not wish to go any farther, saying his doing so would be contrary to the Mudir's orders, and that he was tired. He wished, however, to speak to General Earle, and would come across next day, bringing Abu Bekr and Wad el Turki.

He could not bring Omar, as he had run away.

5th Feb.

On the morning of the 5th General Earle sent over to say, through Colvile, that he was sorry the Vakeel found it inconvenient, but must insist on his coming over and accompanying the General to Salamat. In reply, the Vakeel wrote a letter saying his advancing to Salamat would be useless, as he did not know the country; that he had orders from the Mudir to collect taxes at Hamdab and in the cataracts by the help of the Mudir's troops; that if he advanced to Salamat, their collection would be delayed. He could not disobey the Mudir's orders; and he thought his remaining where he was with the troops would have a good effect, preventing the Monassir from returning.

General Earle still insisting upon his point, the Vakeel at last gave way, consenting to bring his troops over, and to accompany the General, but asserting it would be impossible for him to start until the 8th. General Earle then consented to give him an interview, and he came over to our camp. He protested with such apparent show of reason the utter uselessness of his going to Salamat, that General Earle consented to allow him to remain at Birti with the Mudir's troops, on condition that they crossed over on the morrow. To this the Vakeel consented promptly; and General Earle telegraphed to Lord Wolseley, asking him to urge the Mudir to insist on their remaining at Birti, at least till we should reach Abu Hamed.

With him the Vakeel had brought Abu Bekr, Suleiman Wad Gamr's uncle, and Wad el Turki; and they now remained in our camp. It was known that neither Abu Bekr nor Omar had been on friendly terms with Naaman, Suleiman's father, and they were not supposed to be on friendly terms with Suleiman himself; but a very compromising letter was found on Abu Bekr's person, written shortly after the murder by Suleiman, bidding Abu Bekr come to the council to be held, and speaking of having been occupied with the disposal of the prisoners from the steamer. However, Abu Bekr had come in under a promise of safety; and as he was not actively a participator in the murder, we were able to treat him kindly, and use him as a guide.

Abd el Rahman Wad el Turki was a sheikh of the Shagiyeh tribe. He had fought against the Mudir's troops at Debbeh and at Korti, having raised a small force. After the defeat at Korti, he had retired to the rocks above Edermih cataract, and had collected another force there. He had remained there till our advance, when he retired to Birti, and joined the Robatab under Moussa, bringing with him a contingent of about 100 men. He was a great partisan of the Mahdi.

Colonel Butler's reconnaissance reports having arrived during the night of the 4th. General Earle informed him, on the morning of the 5th, that he did not wish any advance in boats beyond Castle Camp until the two channels in front had been more thoroughly examined. "Lieut.-Colonel Alleyne," the instructions run, "should push boat-reconnaissance up both channels until he has discovered which is the best, and should examine the ground with a view to sites for camping, while you are making an extended reconnaissance towards the front." The Black Watch and remainder of the Staffords were sent on to Castle Camp, and Colonel Butler was told to order the advance of the Staffords on the following day to such point as he might consider best after reconnaissance and consultation with Alleyne. Butler was requested to make his reconnaissance early, so that his report might arrive before sundown, as no further orders would be issued till it arrived. With General Earle's memorandum, a boy, who had been captured in the Mahdi's uniform, and who said that he had deserted from the rebel camp at Shukook, was sent to act as a guide.

While the Staffords and Black Watch

were advancing to Castle Camp, the Cornwalls were arriving at Birti; and as they arrived, they were employed completing the destruction of the houses, palm-trees, and *sakyehs* of Suleiman Wad Gamr, his uncle Omar, and other prominent rebels. Nothing is easier than to destroy a *sakyeh*, its timber and rope burning freely. We found that by an occasional charge of guncotton, and by the free use of pickaxes, we could rapidly level the largest mud-built house to the ground. But the destruction of palm-trees is a difficult matter. The tough fibrous bark blunts the axes, and the tree will not burn freely; nevertheless some 280 date-palms were cut down or utterly destroyed by fire.

The Commissariat continued their search for grain; and it was reported to me that our horses were now rationed with grain up to the 6th March, and our natives with flour to 23d March, without counting six tons of unground wheat to be used for either natives or horses as most required. From

Hamdab to Birti no supplies of any kind, except growing forage, had been obtainable either by capture or purchase. The country had been a desolate waste; the people had buried their grain in the desert, and driven off their cattle. By no offers could they be induced to bring even milk for sale, and by no promise of wage could they be tempted to engage in our service as labourers.

That afternoon, about four o'clock, a cipher-telegram arrived from General Wood, who, we thus learned, was acting as Chief of the Staff in place of Sir R. Buller. General Earle and I deciphered it together. It ran thus: "4th Feb., 8.50 P.M.—I am ordered by Lord Wolseley to inform you that, to his deep regret, Khartoum was found by Wilson to be in possession of enemy. Wilson in returning was wrecked, but steamer has gone for him, and there is no apparent danger for him. You are to halt where you are until further orders."

It is needless to say what we felt. Any

thought for ourselves was swallowed up in grief for what we could only interpret to mean Gordon's certain death. Both of us felt, too, how great the shock would be to Lord Wolseley; and to me there was a peculiar sting in the fact of this blow coming upon the anniversary of the capture of Coomassie. But action had to be at once taken, and immediate orders were sent to Colonel Butler that none of his troops were to move without further orders,—that he was to patrol with small bodies of cavalry only, and hold all his troops ready to move at short notice. Colvile was instructed that the Mudir's troops were not to cross on the morrow; and, convinced in his own mind, as I was in mine, that we should be at once recalled, General Earle would not bring the Gordon Highlanders to Birti, but sent back his aide-de-camp with orders to them to close up at Gamra, construct a zareeba, and halt there till further orders. The officer sent with the order failed to find them, as they had not reached Gamra, where he fully expected they would be; and darkness came on before he could go farther. The order, however, reached them on the following morning early. The contents of the telegram were kept strictly secret, no one but General Earle and myself knowing the cause of the orders to halt.

The evening brought us the report of Colonel Butler's reconnaissance. It has a singular interest by the light of subsequent events. He had proceeded in the direction of the Shukook pass, getting out to the river whenever practicable. He had ascended a high range of hills near the upper end of the large island (Dulka) about six to seven miles distant from his camp—a range which he described as continued across the several branches of the river, its highest point being attained in a large dome-shaped hill on the island of Boni, which overlaps Dulka. For more than an hour previously, the native boy we had sent him had constantly been informing him that Shukook was only a very short distance ahead—on several occasions pointing out what he called the entrance to the pass, amid the rugged surrounding rocks. Now, however, from the top of the hill he pointed out a place two miles distant as the real Shukook, and asserted that a lower range lying between him and it was immediately over the enemy's camp. Colonel Butler had found one or two sites which would do for a camp. The ridge which he had ascended was that on which, five days later, we fought the action of Kirbekan.

Alleyne had proceeded up the southern channel to the foot of the rapids, and then walked on the shore of the island nearly two miles farther. He pronounced the channel practicable. The northern channel was a maze of islands, rocks, and rapid water.

In acknowledging his instructions not to move till further orders, Butler reported later that his camel-corps patrol had fallen in with the enemy, exchanged shots, brought in a prisoner, and captured some camels, goats, and cattle. We afterwards found they had come across a party of armed villagers tending their flocks in a desert wady.

Before the arrival of the telegram telling us of the fall of Khartoum, a long telegram had been sent to Lord Wolseley detailing the position of the troops and the latest news of the enemy. General Earle said in this that he did not anticipate resistance this side of Abu Hamed, and would push on as rapidly as possible, consistently with the necessary precautions. "The road beyond this," he said, "is as bad as the river —a tangled mass of rocks, quite unsuited for mounted troops, and affording neither good anchorage nor good ground for bivouacs." We had informed Colonel Rundle at Korosko of our advance beyond Birti having commenced; and in addition to our previous urgent demands for boat-repairing materials and paint, horse-shoes and nails, to be sent to meet us at Abu Hamed, we now added a moving appeal for trousers, telegraphing: "Men's and many officers' trousers in rags; not sufficient for decency."

Lord Wolseley was now informed that his telegram had been received, and that his instructions were being carried out; and Rundle was advised that the probable date of our arrival at Salamat, which we had given as the 10th February, must now be postponed.

6th Feb. Early on the 6th I rode over to Colonel Butler's camp, and, by General Earle's permission, told him, under the seal of secrecy, the contents of yesterday's telegram. General Earle rode back to Gamra and visited the Gordon Highlanders.

All the troops had a day of thorough rest, much needed after the unending labours of the past fortnight. It gave them the opportunity of washing their clothes and trying to patch the particoloured rags they were wearing as trousers. General Earle talked over with me the arrangements to be made for the return to Korti, which we confidently expected would be ordered; and we sent a party of the Egyptian camel corps back to Abu Dom to act as carriers of messages, requesting the commandants there to send

HALT, AND ADVANCE OF THE ENEMY. 133

us all messages from Lord Wolseley in duplicate — one copy by two of our own camel-men, one copy by a native messenger. And as our stay at Birti might possibly be prolonged, we made sanitary arrangements for supply of water, &c., as for a standing camp.

In the evening Colvile reported that a man had just come in with the news that the enemy, who were in Shukook, had advanced to Kirbekan; that they were not a thousand strong, and had about 150 rifles. They had no outposts at night, but sent out a patrol before daylight. He said they had chosen their present camp as being easier to escape from than Shukook in case of defeat. This information was at once sent to Colonel Butler.

On the 7th the troops were employed in improving the sanitary condition and watering arrangements of the camps. A quantity of grain was discovered by our foraging-parties on Ishishi island, and was brought over to our camp. We had now not only full loads

7th Feb.

of grain for all our camels, but were able out of the surplus to issue a small grain-ration to the camels which had hitherto been subsisting on growing crops only. Our camels were in fair condition, but from want of sufficient work were becoming soft, and the saddle-galls from which these unfortunate animals seem seldom or never free were in consequence not so healthy. We found it necessary to exercise the camels regularly, which had a better effect on their health than even the issue of grain. Butler sent out patrols to the scene of the camel corps skirmish of the 5th, without finding any trace of the enemy.

8th Feb. On the morning of the 8th we sent to the Chief of the Staff a telegram stating the exact state of our supplies, based upon returns obtained during the halt. We told him that the total strength drawing rations last night was 2966 officers and men, and fixed the exact number of days' supply of each article remaining for that number; and we requested him so to arrange that the supplies sent by Rundle to Korosko should equalise the various articles of food. We added that we had thirty days' grain for our 140 horses, but none for our 580 camels; that the latter had hitherto done well on the green forage of the country, but that a prolonged halt would make it very difficult to feed them. Soap we especially asked for to be sent up by first convoy. We had only thirty days' supply remaining; and many of the boats were full of lice, which were infesting the clothes of the men, and in some cases of the officers.

CHAPTER VIII.

KIRBEKAN—RECONNAISSANCE AND PREPARATION.

8th Feb. At 8 A.M. on Sunday the 8th, General Earle received a message from General Wood, dated 1 A.M., 7th: "Lord Wolseley," it said, "is communicating with Government as to future operations, but he wishes you to push on to Abu Hamed, and await further orders there."

Orders were at once issued and despatched for the Gordons to advance immediately by the northern channel to Birti, and for the Staffords; covered by the mounted troops, to advance from Castle Camp to a point to be selected by Colonel Butler. General Earle did not wish to commit more than

RECONNAISSANCE AND PREPARATION. 137

one battalion to the rapids, until their nature was more thoroughly known, and therefore he left the Black Watch at Castle Camp. Wishing to close up the Gordons nearer to the Cornwalls, he left the latter also for the day at Birti. The Black Watch and a wing of the Cornwalls were ordered to advance on the 9th, and the Mudir's troops to cross over to the left bank.

I rode over with the orders to Castle Camp, and found the men in their red coats, after church parade. Within half an hour Alleyne and the first boats were off, and the cavalry scouts were advancing along the bank.

Butler, taking command of the whole advanced guard, left the Staffords at the head of the first rapid, and directed Colonel Eyre to make his camp on Dulka island. He then advanced with Major Flood and twenty Hussars along the left bank. At 2.30 P.M. his scouts fell in with the enemy, posted on some rocky ground, all of which had been patrolled by our mounted troops on the 5th.

Their right rested on the river, and they were dotted about clumps of rock commanding the track by which the cavalry were advancing. Our men took up a position opposite them and fired a few volleys, which made them leave the front faces of the rocky knolls, but they still held their sides and summits. About 4 P.M. four exploring boats arrived by river just below the cavalry, and Butler landed two boats' crews and fired some volleys. Colonel Butler estimated those who had shown themselves as about 200 in number. Only about ten rifles had opened fire, but he had seen many spear-heads. At the approach of sunset Butler retired to Castle Camp, the enemy following him as far as the most advanced position which he had held. The boats fell back to Colonel Eyre's camp on Dulka island.

Colonel Butler reported the position occupied by the enemy as being about two miles from Colonel Eyre's camp on Dulka island, with the river between; and he considered that the Staffords could be moved to the spot where he engaged the enemy in less than two hours, and the Black Watch from Castle Camp in six hours. Colonel Butler said that he would cover the ground for the Staffords landing next day with his mounted troops, and then move the battalion to the left bank, bringing the Black Watch also to the same place, unless otherwise ordered. He asked for two guns to be sent early next day to Castle Camp; and in his report stated that the enemy's right and rear was within easy range of Dulka island, so that guns taken across the river by boat, and carried about two miles along the island, could take the position in reverse. He sent his staff officer, Lieutenant Pirie, with the report.

On receipt of this report at 10 P.M., and after questioning Lieutenant Pirie, General Earle decided that he would himself reconnoitre the position on the following day. He ordered the two guns asked for to Castle Camp, but did not wish them sent over to

Dulka island. He told Colonel Butler that he would leave Birti at 6.30 A.M. for Castle Camp, and directed that an officer should be left there to guide him to the position where he would find Colonel Butler. He approved of the proposal to move the Staffords and Black Watch to the open ground in rear of the position opposite the enemy occupied by the cavalry; and impressed the importance of great care in effecting the crossing of the Staffords, so that it should be impossible for them to be attacked while landing, in case the enemy should advance and compel our cavalry to retire.

9th Feb. On the morning of the 9th, the following instructions were sent to Colonel Colvile: the Mudir's troops, after crossing the river, were to take up a position out of rifle-range of our Birti camp. Headquarters were about to advance, but half a battalion of the Cornwalls would remain at Birti, where the Gordons were expected to arrive that day. Should they do so, all our troops would clear out of Birti on the morning of the

10th, and Colonel Colvile should himself then join General Earle's headquarters. Before leaving, Colvile was to inform the Vakeel that he and the Mudir's troops were to remain in occupation of the Monassir country till further orders,—General Earle relying upon the Vakeel to obtain and forward to us supplies of cattle and grain, to send us information of the movements and intentions of the enemy, and to forward our messages to and from Abu Dom.

By 11 A.M. the Mudir's troops had crossed and bivouacked opposite their former camp. Shortly after landing, they found the mountain-gun from Colonel Stewart's steamer. It was spiked, and the sight, spokes of one wheel, and cap-squares were missing.

General Earle's start from Birti was somewhat delayed; and when we moved on from Castle Camp, the officer sent to guide us unfortunately could not find the way, and lost himself amongst the rocks, so that we did not reach the ground where the Staffords were to encamp until nearly mid-day.

Meanwhile the mounted troops had pushed forward, and had occupied with their advanced posts the rocky hillocks, or koppies, as they are called in South Africa, which they had occupied yesterday, and found the enemy still in the same position as before. Colonel Butler then sent for the Staffords.

General Earle, accompanied by his staff, then personally examined the enemy's position from the rocks upon which our cavalry vedettes were posted, about 800 yards distant. Immediately in front of us the enemy held some rocky koppies about 50 to 80 feet in height, their right being directly over the river. Between two of these koppies ran the road from Birti to Salamat. We could see that they had built stone sconces, or breastworks, among the rocks, and completely commanded with their rifles both road and river. They must clearly be turned out of that before we could advance to Abu Hamed.

Running parallel to the low rocky koppies

RECONNAISSANCE AND PREPARATION. 143

above-named, but to the enemy's left rear, and some 600 yards behind the koppies, and ending abruptly 600 yards from the river, was a very remarkable ridge about 300 feet high, presenting on the side next to us a steep slope like the moraine of a glacier, out of which at the summit projected a ridge of white marble rocks, as the teeth project from the jawbone of a skeleton. This was the ridge ascended by Colonel Butler on the 5th. All along its summit we could see men with flags and spear-heads moving about among the rocks. Still it was evident that these two positions were not capable of holding a large body of men; and we were disposed to believe them held by an outpost some 300 to 400 strong, and that we should find the enemy emerge in force from behind the hills on our advancing to attack them.

There were four ways of attacking the position. First, the direct attack upon the koppies, aided perhaps by flanking fire from Dulka island. This would involve heavy loss, and would be the least effectual, as the enemy, when beaten, would retreat directly along the river, through the broken ground, to the Shukook pass. Secondly, an advance through the valley, between the range of koppies and the marble-topped high ridge. This would turn the koppies; and General Earle inclined to the belief, in which I shared, that if once the enemy in the koppies found themselves outflanked, and liable to have their retreat cut off, they would retreat. Thirdly, to advance upon the marble-topped ridge, and storm it, bringing fire from it to bear afterwards upon the koppies below, while we sent a force to attack them. Fourthly, provided the country would lend itself to the idea, to move to our right under cover of the broken ground, and march completely round the marble-topped ridge, which was only about a mile long, and move round its rear to the attack both of it and of the koppies. Colonel Butler was sent at 4 P.M. to make a wide detour round the ridge, and see if

RECONNAISSANCE AND PREPARATION. 145

there was a fair road for infantry and camels by which we could thus turn the position. On his return he reported that we could turn the position by an easy march through a wide sandy wady, and that he had noted a road by which we could approach the wady from our camp without exposing ourselves to any great extent. This latter plan of advance was therefore decided upon by the General; and as the enemy did not appear to be in great force, it was resolved to attack him the following morning, with such troops as we had ready to our hand.

Sending over to Castle Camp for the two guns to come on, and also for the senior medical officer, with such assistance as he might require, and having informed him of what was in contemplation, we then proceeded to organise the details for the morrow's fight.

By sunset the whole of the Staffords, with two sections of the field-hospital, and the headquarters and seven companies of the

Black Watch, had reached their bivouac, a short mile from the enemy's position. One company of the Black Watch was absent. Having taken the wrong channel, and been fired upon from the right bank, it had returned to Castle Camp, and bivouacked there with the wing of the Cornwalls, who arrived there from Birti. The two guns arrived, and the senior medical officer, with his staff and certain necessary appliances; and the following dispositions for the attack were made.

One company of the Black Watch, under Lieut.-Colonel Eden, with Major Sandwith as his staff officer, was to remain in the zareeba, to guard the boats and baggage. All infantry baggage to be packed in the boats by 6.30 A.M.; all other baggage and baggage-animals to be parked on the low shore, in front of the boats. All headquarter servants, departmental and unarmed men, to remain with the baggage. The boat of the Royal Navy, with its Gatling gun so disposed as to sweep the shore and river up-stream, to be under Lieut.-Colonel Eden's command.

The Staffords and six companies Black Watch, with the two guns, to parade in sufficient time to march off the ground at seven o'clock. Troops in red, Highlanders in kilts. The men to breakfast before parade, and carry one day's rations of meat and biscuit. All water-bottles to be full on marching off. Each man to carry sixty rounds of ammunition, and each battalion to have two camels, each carrying four boxes of reserve ammunition, making 4800 rounds of reserve ammunition for each battalion. The guns to have two ammunition-camels for each gun. Commanding officers, two wing field-officers, and the adjutant of each battalion, to be mounted.

Each battalion to have eight stretchers carried by sixteen of its unarmed men, with four men in reserve as bearers. A detachment of the field-hospital, with three camels carrying surgical and hospital equipment, to parade with the infantry; also two camels to carry water for the field-hospital.

The Hussars and camel corps to parade separately under Colonel Butler.

General Brackenbury, Major Boyle, Major Slade, Captain Beaumont, and Lieutenant St Aubyn to accompany General Earle. All other staff officers to remain with the baggage, except Lieut.-Colonel Alleyne, who was instructed to take command of two companies of the Staffords and the two guns, and to occupy with them the rocky position held yesterday by our cavalry outposts, and to hold the enemy in check in front, attracting their attention in that direction while our flank movement was in progress.

During the afternoon the enemy opened fire from a small island above Dulka island, and one of their shots having struck one of our vedettes, a company of the Staffords was sent across in boats to occupy the island and bivouack there. To reach the island, the boats had to ascend a nasty rapid just opposite our bivouac. All fires were put out at "lights out," and it was ordered that none should be lit before *réveillé* on the following day.

About 3 P.M. a telegram arrived from Lord Wolseley to the following effect— dated 9 A.M., 8th : The Government have decided that the Mahdi's power at Khartoum must be overthrown. This most probably means a campaign here next cold weather, and certainly the retention in the Soudan of all troops now here. A strong force of all arms goes as soon as possible to Suakim to crush Osman Digma. We must now take Berber. Buller will now take Metemmeh. Let me know early the date you calculate upon reaching Berber, so that Buller's force may co-operate with you.

At 5.45 P.M. a long letter arrived from Lord Wolseley to General Earle, dated 2 P.M., 7th. It was almost entirely in cipher, and I sat up till late in the night deciphering its contents. In it Lord Wolseley informed General Earle of the questions he had addressed to the Cabinet, the replies he had received, and his further queries. It amplified the contents of his telegram received that afternoon. It told us that he had not yet heard of Wilson's safety; and in it there was this sentence: " I congratulate you upon the progress you have made, although I am naturally very sorry the enemy have not tested the temper of your steel. However, let us hope their courage may be stiffened by the fall of Khartoum, and that you may strike them hard yet before you reach Berber." Hope soon to be realised!

General Earle talked this letter over with me until a very late hour, and decided not to reply to it till after the action of the morrow. Two of our spies came in, and professed to have been unable to see any trace of the enemy in the position they had held during the day; and we retired to rest, half fearing they might again give us the slip, as they had done ten days before at Birti. But we were needlessly anxious. We did not then know that their courage had been stiffened — that they had heard of the fall of Khartoum.

CHAPTER IX.

KIRBEKAN—THE FIGHT.

10th Feb.

THE night passed without incident. At the earliest dawn our cavalry vedettes were again in their position of yesterday, and as soon as the growing daylight enabled them to see clearly, they reported the enemy still in position—good news which soon spread through the camp. The men were tired of the delays caused by the precautions necessary in the presence of an enemy who escaped just as we were within striking distance; and those holding responsible positions in the force felt it to be of the utmost importance to meet the enemy soon, and get the chance of teaching them a lesson which would prevent their meeting

THE FIGHT.

us again for some time, thus clearing the way for our advance to the main objective of our column—Berber.

The company on outpost-duty at Dulka island was recalled, baggage was parked according to orders, the naval boat was placed in position, the camels were loaded to accompany the column. The men breakfasted and fell in on parade, looking smart and thoroughly workmanlike. After inspection, Lieut.-Colonel Eden's company of the Black Watch was set to work forming a small zareeba; two companies of the Staffordshire Regiment were told off to escort the two guns under Lieut.-Colonel Alleyne; and as soon as we saw the dispositions for defence of the zareeba fairly complete, and Alleyne's two companies and guns marched off to occupy the ground held by our cavalry outposts, with orders not to open fire till we had reached the outer flank of the great ridge round which we were to move, the column marched off. It was then about a quarter past seven. Just before we left the zareeba, General Earle directed me to send back to inform the English correspondent of a foreign newspaper, who had made his way up with the Gordon Highlanders, that, owing to the necessity for economising all food for man and beast, and in view of all spare whaler accommodation being required for transport of sick, he could not allow any civilian correspondents to accompany the column.

We marched in line of half-battalion columns, at an interval of two companies, the Staffords (six companies) leading, the Black Watch (six companies) following. Company stretcher-bearers followed their own companies. The field-hospital camels and reserve small-arm ammunition camels (nine and one spare), were massed between the Staffords and Black Watch, and moved with the left column. The General's object in this formation was to enable each column to take advantage of practicable ground for marching as long as we were moving over the rocks, but at the same time to be able, by closing the columns together, to get rapidly into formation ready to form square, or rather oblong, with the stretcher-bearers and camels inside.

Colonel Butler led the column. The first mile of our road lay in a north-easterly direction over broken but hard ground; then we reached a wide wady of loose deep sand, in which progress was slow and fatiguing, and followed it till we reached the farthest end of the marble-topped ridge. We then, at about half-past eight, halted for a few minutes, allowing a few men to fall out. Not a shot had been fired at us as yet, though our column must have been visible from the ridge at more than one point in its march. While here we heard Alleyne's guns open fire.

Our front as we marched had been covered by the cavalry; our left flank by the Egyptian camel corps, who lined the edge of the broken ground opposite to the high ridge. Colonel Butler now went on with the cavalry scouts, and just as we were about to continue our march, sent back to say that the enemy were in sight on some low rocky hills, to the number of two or three hundred, and immediately afterwards a second message to say the enemy were retiring. We now marched round the eastern end of the ridge, and turning sharp to the left, marched through a rocky valley in the direction of the river, with the high ridge on our left. In front of us was a low rocky range running at right angles to the high ridge on which Colonel Butler had seen the enemy. The enemy now opened fire on us from the high ridge at about 9.15 A.M., and we had two or three men hit. General Earle, after a short farther advance, halted the column under cover, and sent forward one company of the Staffords to the low range in front, and another company (C) to line the rocks on our left, and keep down the fire from the high ridge. The enemy not appearing immediately in front, the column advanced about 300 yards into a valley with rocky ridges on

THE FIGHT.

every side, leaving C Company of the Staffords engaged with the enemy on the high ridge. The fire from this ridge now becoming hotter, General Earle directed Colonel Eyre to take two companies of his regiment and endeavour to take the ridge by its western shoulder. They advanced under a heavy fire, and climbed about one third of the way up the shoulder, till they reached a cluster of rocks under which they obtained partial shelter.

At the same time two companies of the Black Watch descended the rocky ridge to our right front, from whence the river was visible about six hundred yards away; and we could see parties of the enemy making their way to it, and swimming over to the opposite bank. It being then evident that the only serious opposition we had to expect was from the enemy remaining on the high marble-topped ridge, and on the koppies, whence fire was now opened on us, General Earle ordered two companies of the Black Watch to move to their right front towards the river-bank, and establish themselves there, so as to prevent all retreat in this direction; and the three remaining companies of the Staffords and the four remaining companies of the Black Watch to advance and swing round to the left, so as to face the koppies.

It now became evident, from the fire which was directed upon us from the koppies, that the enemy had a considerable body of riflemen in position there, and the two companies of the Black Watch which had been sent down to the river were ordered to advance in line along the river-bank towards the koppies, clearing it of the enemy.

The remainder of the Black Watch and Staffords took up a position on the rocks, at about 800 yards, and brought a heavy fire to bear upon the koppies. Little by little they advanced from one vantage-point to another, till they attained a position on the nearest rocks to the koppies, about 400 yards distant. Between them and the koppies there was now only open ground, swept by the enemy's fire.

General Earle now ordered the two companies of the Black Watch nearest the river, who had by this time come up abreast of our main position, to advance along the shore of the low Nile, under cover of the high bank, and take the koppie nearest the river from its river flank. A company of the Staffords accompanied them, and advancing rapidly under cover of the river-bank, they seized the lowest rocks and then the summit of this koppie, driving out or killing the rebels who were there. Some of these attempted flight by the river in the direction of Colonel Alleyne's men and our zareeba; a few escaped by swimming, but many were shot down by our men. From the summit of this koppie now in our hands, a flanking fire was brought to bear upon the two main central koppies.

It was now evident that nothing more was to be done but to assault the position, and the order was about to be given when a body of the enemy, one of whom carried a flag, the rest being armed with spears, descended boldly from the heights in front, and charged towards the nearest companies of the Black Watch, which were somewhat advanced towards our left front, under Colonel Green. The troops never moved, but the gallant Arabs were received with so withering a fire from all sides that those who were not killed turned and fled towards the river. A few gained it. Our men, far from fearing the rush, stood up to meet it, in some cases even advanced; and they could with difficulty be restrained from leaving the ranks to follow the fugitives along the river.

This episode over, the order for the assault was given, and well responded to. I had myself previously carried the orders to the troops on the koppie by the river to advance simultaneously with the front assault, and had returned to General Earle to the front of the position previous to the enemy's charge. General Earle ordered

THE FIGHT.

the assault to be made; and then, with pipes playing, the Black Watch charged over the open ground and stormed the koppies, not stopping till they had crowned the highest rocks. The troops on the river-side koppie also well carried out their orders, advancing from the flank and seizing the koppie nearest to them. Such of the enemy as still remained fought to the last, and were killed to a man.

The assault was over, and the two main koppies were in our hands; the troops were searching the sconces and holes among the rocks; and there was, as there must always be after such an effort, some need to collect them and form them up for fresh work. Between the crests of the two main koppies there was a depression forming a small flat plateau, on which was built a stone hut some ten feet square, with a thatched roof. General Earle was engaged in forming up the men in the ranks on this plateau, not more than ten yards from the hut, when a sergeant of the Black Watch said, "There are a lot of men in that hut, and they have just shot one of our men." General Earle ordered the roof to be set on fire; but on its being said that there was a quantity of ammunition in the hut, he ordered the roof to be pulled down, and himself approached the hut. I was close to him, and said, "Take care, sir; the hut is full of men." Our men had set the roof on fire, and my attention was attracted for a moment by seeing a native who rushed out from the side door of the hut bayoneted by one of our men. As I turned my head back towards the General, I saw him fall, shot through the head from a small square window in the hut, close to which he had approached. He lived only a few minutes, tended to the last by his aide-de-camp Lieutenant St Aubyn, and by the senior medical officer, Surgeon-Major Harvey.

The command having now devolved upon me, I directed two companies of the Black Watch to remain as a picket on the koppies; and I had sent to the Staffords

THE FIGHT.

with a view to assembling them, when it was brought to my knowledge that the two companies of the Staffords sent to take the high ridge had failed as yet to reach higher than the cluster of rocks about one-third of the way up; that Colonel Eyre had been killed, shot through the heart; that Captain Horsburgh and Lieutenant Colborne had been severely wounded; that their loss in men had been considerable; that their ammunition was exhausted, except four rounds per man, which they had reserved; and that the enemy was still holding the ridge. Assembling, therefore, four companies of the Black Watch as a reserve at the foot of the koppies, I sent for Lieutenant-Colonel Beale, upon whom the command of the Staffords had devolved, and instructed him to take the remainder of his regiment, reinforce the two companies on the hill with troops and ammunition, and with the aid of the company left to watch the hill early in the day, assault and take the position. The order was most admirably carried out. Ascending the steep moraine-like hill by alternate rushes, the Staffords reached the rocky summit, and bayoneted the enemy, who remained there fighting to the very end.

It was now about one o'clock, and the enemy were driven from their last position. Meanwhile, early in the day, Colonel Butler, with the few Hussars at his disposal, had struck the river above the point where we first gained it, and had pursued scattered groups of Arabs who were retreating along the main river track. Half an hour later he gained the entrance to the Shukook pass, and in the centre of the rocky gorge there came upon the enemy's deserted camp, where he captured a number of standards, and some camels and donkeys. While there the enemy opened fire upon the Hussars from the surrounding hills, but without causing any casualties among our men. Colonel Butler sent back for camelmen to drive in the animals captured: the message did not reach me till after the fight, and the camel corps having then been

THE FIGHT.

fighting for the whole morning, I instructed Colonel Butler to return with the cavalry to camp. He had already anticipated this order, driving back some of the animals with the Hussars.

The Egyptian camel corps under Major Marriott had done excellent service. They had at the commencement of the day taken up a position in front of the high ridge, and protected the flank of the infantry in its advance. In that position they remained throughout the day, assisting by their fire to keep down the fire from the heights, and shooting, or in some instances pursuing and capturing, the rebels who attempted to escape towards the east, along the southern slope of the hill. Their conduct was witnessed by the Staffords, who remained so long upon the shoulder of the hill, and was the theme of much praise. When the Staffords stormed the hill one Egyptian soldier charged up the hill, all alone, on their extreme right—a most gallant feat. They had two men killed and one wounded.

Leaving, as already said, two companies of the Black Watch on the summit of the koppies, and sending two companies to bivouac on a high Nile island at the head of the rapid, about a mile and a half up the river, I ordered the remainder of the troops back to camp.

During the action the wounded had been collected, as far as possible, by the stretcher-bearers into groups under shelter from fire; dressing-stations had been established at successive points as we moved on; and restoratives, such as beef-tea prepared on the field, champagne, and brandy, were administered to the wounded during and after the action. Owing to the nature of the ground, both medical officers and wounded had been frequently exposed to considerable cross-fire. The medical officers of corps had accompanied their men into action, and the medical officers of the dressing-station gave their services freely wherever most required. As soon as the action was over, additional men were told off as stretcher-bearers, and the wounded were brought into our camp. The bodies of General Earle, Colonel Eyre, and Colonel Coveney, were conveyed back to our camp; the other brave dead were buried together by the river-bank, near the field where they had fallen.

At sunset the bodies of General Earle, Colonel Eyre, and Colonel Coveney were buried side by side in deep graves near the foot of a solitary palm-tree; and the hill of Kirbekan echoed back the boom of the minute-guns paying their solemn tribute to the memory of three soldiers, each a type of what the English officer should be.

Orders were then issued for the half-battalion of the Cornwalls, which had arrived in camp during the day, together with the two companies of the Staffords and the two companies of the Black Watch which had not been engaged in the flank march, to advance by river in the morning, and occupy the position at the head of the rapid, relieving the two companies of the

Black Watch there, and for the remainder of the Cornwalls who had reached Castle Camp to come on to our camp. I wished now to put the Cornwalls and Gordons in front; but the latter, to my disappointment, had not got farther than Birti, their progress through the northern channel of the Rahami cataract having been, owing to the falling Nile, slower than that of the other troops who had traversed the same passage. They were ordered to come on as soon as possible.

It was a busy night. There was much to be thought of and arranged. I sent off a telegraphic summary and a written despatch, and a letter to Lord Wolseley, in which I said, "Our troops having turned them out of these positions, must have a great effect upon the spirit of the enemy. I sincerely trust it may prevent our having to fight our way to Abu Hamed, as if we have many such fights as to-day, we shall be seriously embarrassed how to carry on our wounded. If it enables us to pass the Shukook pass, which is still before us, and to get through the rapids ahead without more fighting, it will indeed be a valuable day for us."

We had not purchased our victory cheaply. General Earle, Colonel Eyre, Colonel Coveney, and nine men killed; four officers and forty-four men wounded, made a total of sixty,—a serious loss in our little force of twelve hundred. It had been most difficult to estimate either the enemy's strength or his loss with accuracy. I do not believe that when we marched to attack the position there were more than about eight hundred men holding it. Half of these made their escape before we attacked; a few more during the fight. The remainder were simply desperate men, resolved to fight to the last, and to sell their lives dearly. They were in what might fairly have been called an impregnable position, and they were thoroughly well armed,—a position out of which they could not have been dislodged by any but first-rate troops. We have all heard of "a position which ten men could hold against a thousand." I honestly confess that the expression conveys exactly what was in my mind when first I saw the hills we had to attack.

In my despatch written that night, I gave the probable loss of the enemy as not less than a hundred and fifty. This I altered to two hundred after going over the ground next day with Colonel Butler. We counted sixty dead bodies on the main koppies, sixty-five on the razor-backed ridge; others were lying below; there were many whom we could not have seen; many had been shot crossing the river: and I am satisfied now that the larger figure does not overstate the enemy's loss.

Not less valuable than the effect of this action upon the enemy's *morale* was its effect upon the spirits of our own men. It inspired them with great confidence. The

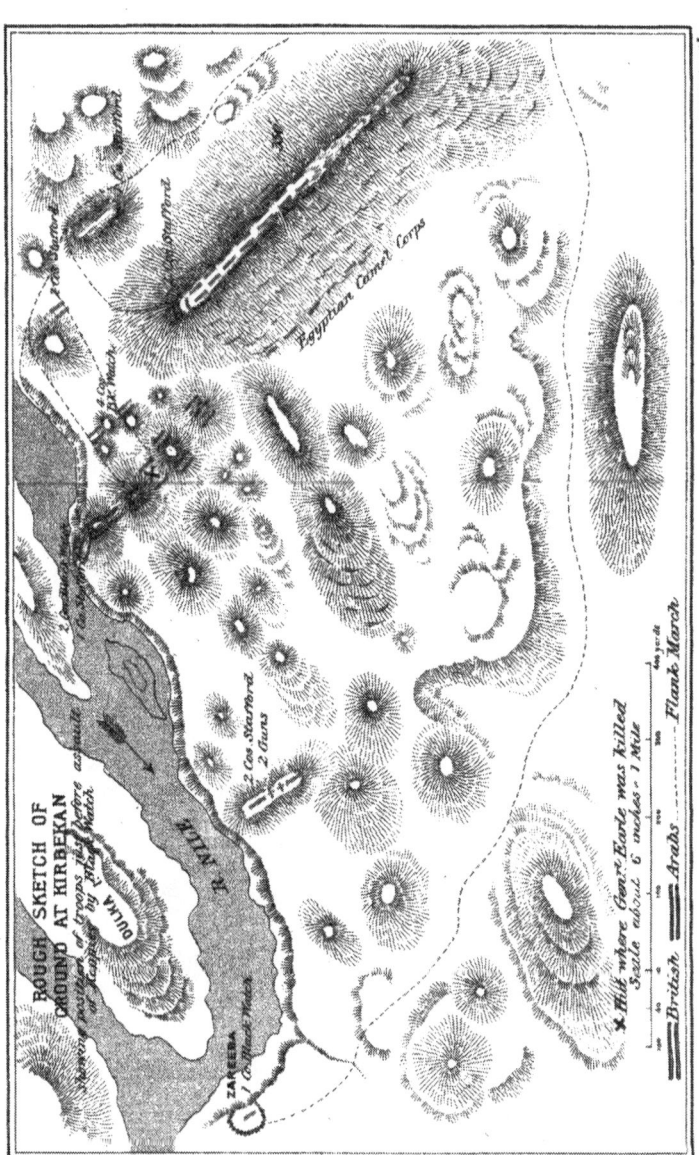

idea that unless in square formation they could not stand against Arabs had been to a certain extent prevalent : to-day the troops had learnt that they could beat their enemy in hand-to-hand combats in the rocks, fighting in loose order.

CHAPTER X.

THE SHUKOOK PASS.

11th Feb. On the morning of the 11th, the troops began to pass through the troublesome rapid commencing opposite our camp, and a wing of the Cornwalls, two companies of the Black Watch, and two of the Staffords — all troops which had not been engaged on the previous day — reached the high Nile island at Kirbekan, and camped there, relieving the companies of the Black Watch who had bivouacked there the preceding night. The mounted troops covered the advance, and Butler reconnoitred to the entrance of, and some distance into, the Shukook pass, seeing no sign of any enemy. The other wing of the Cornwalls, the artillery and convoy, arrived in our camp opposite Dulka island, and the Gordons reached Castle Camp.

Now was the time when a strong force of cavalry would have been invaluable. To push on after the enemy with cavalry, and at once seize and hold the upper end of the Shukook pass, before he could rally from his defeat, was the proper course to pursue. It could not be done with infantry, for the infantry were tied to their boats, and every man who marched a yard beyond his boat, had to be marched back again to it sooner or later. As for mounted troops, all that could be spared, after leaving the strictly necessary guards with the main camp, the artillery and convoy, were about sixty Hussars, and forty to fifty of the Egyptian camel corps; and to push on so small a force to encamp at the far side of this long and difficult pass without any infantry support, would have been to court disaster. The mounted troops, therefore, fell back to the bivouac at Kirbekan.

Slade examined nine prisoners whom we had taken in the action of yesterday, and reported that, from their statements, the enemy who had held the position consisted of 400 men of the Robatab tribe, under Sheikh Moussa Wad Abu Hegel; 200 men from Berber, under Sheikh Ali Wad Hussein and Hamid Lekalik, cousin and brother respectively of Abdul Majid Wad el Lekalik; 300 of the Monassir tribe, under Sheikh el Hagid; and several slaves and villagers from their lands,—making a total of about 1500 to 2000 men, of whom the Robatab and Berber men alone had held the position so stoutly defended. All the sheikhs abovenamed, with the exception of El Hagid, were killed during the action, Moussa's body having been identified by one of the prisoners. The main camp of the enemy was at the upper end of the Shukook pass, the camp taken by our mounted troops at the lower end of the pass being only an advanced post. The prisoners stated that neither Suleiman Wad Gamr nor Abdul

Majid Wad el Lekalik had been present at the action, the former being at Salamat, the latter at the main camp. They said that their losses had been very heavy, only those who escaped by swimming the river having been saved. They all agreed in stating that after the enemy left Birti, they had retired to the spot where the main camp now was, at the upper end of the Shukook pass, and that they had returned and occupied the position at Kirbekan on the 6th, strengthening the position by reinforcements from the main camp on the evening of the 9th.

At the Vakeel's request we sent two of our prisoners to be examined by him at Birti, he thinking that he would get more information out of them than we could. His report practically confirmed Slade's: he estimated the numbers present at 2000, and the killed at 700. He expressed his opinion that we should meet with no more opposition till we reached Berber.

The prisoners also said that they had

heard there were 2000 men under Hassan Wad Mahommed at Abu Hamed, consisting of Ababdeh and Robatab men, and men from Berber. They had converted the Government *shoona* (grain-store) into a barrack: it is in the middle of the town, five hundred yards from the river, and has a mud wall ten to twelve feet high, and two feet thick. They had constructed no other defences.

A spy who had been sent from Korti to Berber arrived in our camp, according to his orders, on his way back to Korti. He had left Berber about a week before. This was his account of the state of affairs there. The guns which had been on the left bank at Robush had been removed—one to Metemmeh, and one to the right bank at Berber. Mohammed el Kheir had moved his own property across the river to the right bank. Many Berber men had been killed in the fight at Abu Klea, and the news of that fight had spread terror through the town. Most of the men now at Berber were Magrafaab Jaalins. The Hadendowas and the Bisharin Arabs from the Atbara had been asked to come and fight the English, but had refused. Nour Anga, the governor of Metemmeh, had sent to the Mahdi for ammunition, but it had been refused to him. The gun at Berber was out of order. Food was scarce in Berber, and the spy professed himself convinced that, when the English approached, the Jaalins between Berber and Metemmeh would surrender.

By this time I had learnt by experience that native reports might generally be classed under two heads: those of spies, who said what they thought we should like to hear; and those of professed deserters, which were intended to frighten us. We had constantly heard from our spies that the tribes were frightened; that the Mahdi's troops were deserting him; that this tribe and that had refused to join him; that the enemy would not fight, but join us when we advanced. Of these this spy's account was a specimen. We as constantly heard from men who came to us, professing to be deserters, greatly exaggerated accounts of the enemy's numbers and determination to fight. Of these, the deserter who had come in to our camp at Mishami was a specimen. In fact, the only information of value was what our own reconnaissance told us, and what was supplied to us through Colvile by the Vakeel.

That evening Colonel Butler rode back to my camp, bringing with him an Arabic document. It had been found, he told me, by a private of the Cornwalls in the saddle-bag of a donkey, which was found grazing on the bank near the Kirbekan camp. There being a very strict column-order that all papers of every description found anywhere were to be preserved and sent to the intelligence officer, this paper had been kept for that purpose. But in the meantime it had been shown to the interpreter of the battalion, and rumour had spread through the camp that Khartoum had been taken and Gordon killed.

THE SHUKOOK PASS. 179

I sent for my interpreter and translator, who spoke and wrote French but not English. On my showing him the paper, and asking him what it contained, he answered: "Très mauvaises nouvelles; il dit que le Mahdi a pris Khartoum, et que Gordon a été tué." I made him translate it, and from his translation I again made the following version, which I at once sent to Abu Dom to be telegraphed to Lord Wolseley:—

Copy of a letter received from the Governor-General of Berber to the Governor of the Section.

"In the name of God, &c., from Mohammed el Kheir, Abdullah Khogeali, Emir-General of Berber, to his friend, Abdul Majid Wad el Lekalik, and all his men.—I inform you that to-day after the mid-day prayer we received a letter from the faithful Khalife Abdullah Eben Mohammed, in which he tells us that Khartoum was taken on Monday the ninth Rabi 1302, on the side of El Hauoi, in the following manner. The Mahdi (pray upon (*priez sur*) him, his dervishes, and his troops) advanced against the fortifications, and entered Khartoum in a quarter of an hour. They killed the traitor (*le perfide*) Gordon, and captured the steamers and boats. God has made him glorious; be grateful, and thank and praise God for His unspeakable mercy. I announce it to you. Tell your troops."

The document was dated the thirteenth Rabi, and on it was written, "Received, Friday the twentieth Rabi."

Comparing these dates with the 'Soudan Almanac' prepared in the Intelligence Department in London, we found that the letter announced the fall of Khartoum to have taken place on Monday the 26th January; it had been written at Berber on the 30th January, and received at the Shukook pass on Friday the 6th February. Now we understood why the enemy had returned on that day to Kirbekan, and what had stiffened their courage.

12th Feb. On the 12th the wing of the Cornwalls at Kirbekan camp advanced about a mile through the rapids to the mouth of a broad wady—probably one of the many branches of the Wady el Argu, which runs across the desert from Kirbekan to Abu Egli, on

THE SHUKOOK PASS.

the Nile above Berber; and the wing at Dulka camp closed up upon them, the last boat arriving at 4 P.M. It would have been impossible to advance a whole battalion farther, and it was not desirable to move a small force in boats into the rocky reaches of the Shukook until those reaches were examined, and the pass itself reconnoitred to its farthest end, so that we might ascertain what lay behind, and whether the pass itself was clear. We were evidently now about to become entangled in a long rocky pass both by road and river.

The Engineers and royal naval boat, with two sections of field-hospital, accompanied the Cornwalls. The Staffords closed up at Kirbekan; and three companies succeeded in reaching Wady el Argu camp, but not till very late. Five companies, with two companies Black Watch, remained at Kirbekan, and the Gordons closed up to our camp opposite Dulka island. Owing to the shallowness of the water, and their boats being very heavily laden, they had been obliged to abandon three boats on their way up from Hamdab.

Alleyne reconnoitred a mile and a half up stream, from Wady el Argu to the foot of a very swift rapid, which he reported must be tracked up; and Butler reconnoitred with the mounted troops, making a wide cast out into the desert, and returning through the Shukook pass, without finding any signs of the enemy. He found a site for a camp at the mouth of a wady in the Shukook pass, not far from Jebel Shukook, the mountain which is the one conspicuous feature in the mass of rugged rocks here piled together, and returned to the bivouac at Wady el Argu. Orders were therefore issued for an advance to the Shukook camp on the following day.

In the morning I had received a telegram, addressed to General Earle by the Chief of the Staff, dated the 9th. It informed me that the Government had decided that we were to stay in the Soudan till the Mahdi's power at Khartoum was destroyed. If we could not do this before the hot weather, we must wait until autumn. Buller had left Gakdul on the 8th for Gubat, and would take Metemmeh as soon as the Royal Irish reached Gubat. It was assumed that I could reach Berber on the 28th February, or have reported my proximity to it. Buller would be in the neighbourhood, with four or six guns and about 1500 men, on the left bank. If I did not think I could reach Berber by that date, I was to name a date, in order that Buller might meet me and co-operate in the attack on Berber. The desert road to Gubat would be held, and a garrison left there, with a view to subsequent operations of the united columns against Khartoum, if, as all native report declared to be the case, Gordon was still holding out. I was therefore to push forward with all possible speed compatible with safety. I was to leave a garrison of 200 men at Abu Hamed, instead of 300 as previously ordered, with 250 rounds of ammunition per man, and sixty days' provisions. The telegram further contained orders as to the precautions to be taken by the commandant of the garrison, and other matters not necessary to detail.

To this telegram I replied that I did not think it possible to reach Berber by the 28th February, and that any date given must be pure conjecture, the time being dependent upon condition of unknown rapids and unknown movements of the enemy. I said it was impossible to pass more than one battalion a-day through the rapids here; and if the enemy were holding the Shukook, I must again concentrate the whole or part of my force. When we reached Salamat, I should be able to give an approximate date for reaching Abu Hamed, and at that place an approximate date for reaching Berber. Now I could only say I did not think we could reach the latter place under one month from this date (12th February). I intended to cross over my mounted troops and transport before reaching Abu Hamed.

THE SHUKOOK PASS.

Fresh supplies of boat-repairing material arrived during the day, sent by camel from Korti; they were very urgently needed. Our boats were suffering severely from the shallow and rocky rapids up which they had to be forced. Planks, pitch, paint, and copper nails were conspicuous by their absence; and where a plank was stove in, it had to be repaired by a patch of tin from a biscuit-box, nailed over the leak with iron nails taken from the boxes which contained our food.

Three men of the Staffords died to-day of their wounds. The other wounded of the Staffords had been carried on in their boats, arrangements having been made for their transport, and for the transport of the wounded of the Black Watch by their own regiments. Each wounded man had his boat's number attached to his stretcher, and a medical officer superintended his being placed in the boat. They were to sleep in the boats or in tents pitched on shore, as the surgeon might think best in each case.

In the first instance, the stretchers were placed athwart-ships near the stern, in front of the coxswain; but it was found that the ends of the stretchers were liable to be knocked against in hauling the boats up rapids, or coming in to shore in swift water; and as this annoyed men made nervous by pain and weakness, arrangements were afterwards made for laying the stretchers along fore and aft, on the thwarts, between the rowers. Awnings were spread for wounded men, but were not allowed in any other boats.

We had captured about 140 rifles on the scene of the action, of which the majority had been broken at the time. These broken ones we threw into the middle of the river; but about 40 Remingtons we retained, with the intention of arming our unarmed men with them in case of need; and at our request the Vakeel returned to us 1000 rounds of Remington ammunition, which we had captured at Birti, and handed over to him.

On the 13th the Cornwalls and four com- 13th Feb. panies of the Staffords advanced about five miles, partly through rapids, to the Shukook camp. The rest of the Staffords, the Gordons, and two companies Black Watch, closed up at Wady el Argu, to which I advanced my headquarters.

Alleyne reconnoitred four miles of clear and not very swift water beyond. Through overhanging rocky cliffs, Butler, with the mounted troops, reconnoitred to the upper end of the Shukook pass opposite Uss island. Here there was another rapid, but not so formidable as some we had passed. He reported the country opening out, but no traces of cultivation; and considered that the Cornwalls and the wing of the Staffords from Shukook could reach the foot of the rapid next day, and possibly commence its passage.

The early morning saw the death of Captain Lord Avonmore from enteric fever. He, no less than those who fell at Kirbekan, was killed in action. He had overtaxed his apparently boundless energy; and the exhaustion produced by incessant exposure to the sun, and great physical fatigue, left him too weak to repel the insidious attack of the disease. We laid him by the side of the officers whom we had buried on the 10th; and as we turned away for the last time from those nameless graves, many a strong man's eyes were moist, and many a lip quivered from heartfelt emotion.

To-day the news reached us by telegram from Korti that Sir Charles Wilson and Lieutenant Stuart Wortley had reached Korti on the 9th, with a short account of Lord Charles Beresford's brilliant affair with the enemy. We learnt that half the West Kent Regiment was to leave for Gakdul on the 10th, and that Lord Wolseley would possibly leave for the same place on the 15th.

No information had yet been given to the troops as to the fall of Khartoum; but as the Reuter's telegram which arrived simultaneously with this news alluded to it

THE SHUKOOK PASS.

as a fact established, I thought it desirable, to prevent wild rumours, to circulate the following memorandum throughout the force :—

"From information received from Lord Wolseley, there is reason to fear that the original object of this expedition—namely, the relief of General Gordon—cannot be carried out.

"When Sir Charles Wilson arrived before Khartūm, he found it in the hands of the enemy; and from information derived from a letter captured after the action of Kirbekan, it is believed that Khartūm was taken by the Mahdi on the 26th of January, and that General Gordon was killed.

"Sir Charles Wilson in returning from Khartūm was wrecked. He and his party appear to have taken refuge on an island, whence, according to information received from the Chief of the Staff, they were brought off by a steamer under the command of Captain Lord Charles Beresford, R.N.

"Lord Charles Beresford had a brilliant little engagement with the enemy, who were in position on the bank with four guns. One shot hit the boiler, disabling the steamer till the boiler was repaired, which was done under fire, taking the greater part of the day. One sailor was killed, and Lieutenant Van Koughnet, R.N., wounded, but not dangerously.

"Sir Charles Wilson and Lieutenant Stuart Wortley arrived at Korti on the night of the 10th instant.

"It is understood to be the present intention of her Majesty's Government to break up the Mahdi's power in the Soudan, and a strong force of all arms is proceeding to Souakim to crush Osman Digna.

"Headquarters and three companies of the West Kent Regiment left Korti on the 10th instant for Gakdul.

"Lord Wolseley will probably leave later to join General Buller's force, and co-operate with this column in the capture of Berber."

14th Feb. On the 14th the Cornwalls advanced to and reached the foot of Uss rapid, opposite Little Uss island, entered the rapid, and made some progress through it. Here was the true upper entrance to the Shukook pass, which had evidently been the site of a camp of the enemy. I halted the leading wing of the Staffords at the foot of the rapid, and the Gordons and other wing of

THE SHUKOOK PASS. 191

the Staffords closed up upon them before nightfall. The Black Watch reached Wady el Argu, as did the artillery and convoy.

I moved my headquarters to the foot of Uss rapid. The troopers sent back as guides by Colonel Butler to lead me from our Wady el Argu camp through the Shukook, instead of turning to the right, as they should have done, at the entrance to the pass, took a turn to the left, and involved me and the baggage-convoy in a labyrinth of the wildest description.

The path by which they brought us was utterly unfitted for a track for loaded camels, though practicable enough for horses. We marched for six miles through as bad ground as it was possible to traverse, wedged in between rocks; and it was evidently impossible that this could be what was after all a well-known and much-travelled pass. Inquiries from Abu Bekr, who was in rear with the baggage, satisfied me that there was another road far better, and little, if at all, longer; and I sent back Colonel Colvile with Abu Bekr to Wady el Argu, to lead the convoy by the better route the next day.

Colonel Butler reconnoitred three or four miles beyond the head of Uss rapid, and found swift water but no bad rapid. Cultivation commenced ahead; and there were many mimosa-trees, the ground becoming more open. No signs of any enemy, and all inhabitants fled.

A spy returned from Salamat, which was now only ten miles from our advanced camp, reported that the people had fled on the 12th, carrying all their possessions with them, in the direction of the Robatab country or into the desert. Colonel Butler was therefore instructed to push his mounted troops home into Salamat the following day, and ascertain whether it was still held by the enemy or not.

I was now in a position to place the Gordon Highlanders ahead of the Staffordshire Regiment in the order of march, and accordingly the following orders were issued for the next day's advance :—

"The Cornwalls to continue their advance through Uss rapid, covered by the advance of the mounted troops; the Gordons to enter the Uss rapid, moving in two columns—one by each bank; the Staffords to be in readiness to follow the Gordons; the Black Watch to advance from Wady el Argu to the foot of Uss rapid."

This rapid opposite Uss island, though not marked in any map or mentioned in any account of the river, proved one of the most troublesome obstacles we had yet encountered. Boats had to track singly by the island bank up the last rush of water. The Gordons had passed through the lower 15th Feb. portion of the rapid, and closed up on the rear of the Cornwalls, long before these were all through the upper rush of water. In fact, by 2 P.M. only the Cornwalls and two companies of the Gordons were through the rapid.

Meanwhile Butler reconnoitred with the mounted troops, and at 1.30 P.M. entered the beginning of the long village of Salamat, which extends for some two and a half miles along the left bank opposite the island of Sherri. He found the whole village deserted. He reported that there was another bad rapid opposite Sherari island — but above that, clear water apparently for some miles; and that opposite the upper end of the village of Salamat, the yellow sand of the true right bank of the Nile was again visible.

Alleyne, with the leading boats, reached a small village opposite the island of Shoar, about four miles above the Uss rapid, in four hours from leaving the head of the rapid, and halted there. All boats which had passed through the Uss rapid by 2 P.M., and which could therefore reach the Shoar bivouac before dark, were sent on there.

The remainder of the Gordons were passed through Uss rapid, and encamped on the left bank at its head. The Staffords concentrated on a small sand island at the foot of the bad part of the rapid, ready to commence passing through it at daylight;

and the Black Watch bivouacked in the camp at the foot, occupied by the Staffords and Gordons the preceding night.

Early in the day I had moved my headquarters to the old dervish's camp opposite to the rapid and to the entrance of the Shukook pass, and about noon had the pleasure of seeing the head of the convoy and the battery emerge from the pass. That pass had long been a subject of anxiety to us, and rightly so. In the course of the day I rode back some two or three miles through it, and an uglier place it was difficult to conceive. In some places there was barely room for a loaded camel to pass between the perpendicular rocks; in others, where the path was wider, the rocks had been prepared for defence by loopholed stone sconces, in the same way as the koppies and ridge at Kirbekan. There was no order or regularity in the plan of the rocks. They seemed to have been upheaved as a mass in some great volcanic convulsion, and to have fallen one upon another in every direction, covering a space some six miles long by three or four broad. With our infantry tied to the boats, as it was, and with so small a force of mounted troops, it would have been a most difficult task to dislodge an active and determined enemy from such a position, of which he knew every outlet, and of which we knew nothing. It was an oppressive place to remain in. It had not even the redeeming element of grandeur, such as great massive features give to the most rugged mountain-range. It represented low, sullen savagery. It was typical of the tribe to whom it belonged.

Orders were issued for a general advance of all the boats from their respective positions in the morning; and I was enabled, with a light heart, to report to Lord Wolseley that our cavalry had entered Salamat, and that the convoy was through the Shukook pass.

CHAPTER XI.

SALAMAT—DESTRUCTION OF SULEIMAN WAD GAMR'S PROPERTY.

My report to Lord Wolseley on the 15th was 15th Feb. to the following effect: "Cavalry entered Salamat to-day, and found it deserted. Leading infantry are within five miles of Salamat; but a bad rapid intervenes opposite Sherari island, which will probably require 500 yards' portage. The rapid opposite Uss island is not marked in any map, nor had we any information of its existence; but it takes three days to get the troops through it. Under conditions of exceptionally low Nile and unexpected rapids, any estimate of time must be mere guess-work. I hope I may reach Abu

Hamed in ten days, but do not think I can concentrate there in less than fourteen, as I have all my camels and horses to cross over."

Colonel Butler, in his reconnaissance of the 15th, had reported Sherri island as being richly cultivated, with many houses. Some of the inhabitants had hailed his party across the river, and asked for "grace," exactly in the same way as the inhabitants of Hebbeh had asked for "grace" from Colonel Stewart when his steamer was wrecked there. Butler had replied that grace would be given to all except the murderers of Stewart and his companions; and the islanders replied that they had to consult the rest of their people, and would reply when all our soldiers had arrived at Salamat.

16th Feb. On the 16th the mounted troops advanced and covered the head of Sherari rapid, while the Cornwalls advanced to it and succeeded in passing six companies through, which bivouacked above the rapid.

SULEIMAN'S PROPERTY DESTROYED.

The lower half of this rapid was not difficult when once the channel was known; but there was only one narrow and difficult passage through the upper half. In one place there was only just sufficient water through sunken rocks for a hundred yards. The boats were all taken through by a party of voyageurs. A company of the Gordons, with Captain Peel, was sent to try another channel round Sherari island; but they returned, having lost one boat swamped. The remainder of the Cornwalls and the Gordons bivouacked below the upper portion of the rapid—the Staffords at Shoar, and the Black Watch still at Uss—the river above being too much blocked with boats for them to move during the day. The mounted troops joined the Cornwalls at the head of the rapid. Headquarters bivouacked with the Gordons; and the convoy was brought on to the same place, as it afforded good camping-ground and forage.

In consequence of the attitude of the inhabitants of Sherri island, I sent to them a letter in Arabic, promising that if they would lay down their arms and assist us with supplies, no one should be harmed except the murderers of Colonel Stewart, and that their houses and *sakyehs* should be spared. The letter was delivered on the island.

Orders were issued for all troops to advance on the following day—the cavalry to cover the advance of the Cornwalls; the camel corps to remain in bivouac, and cover the convoy, artillery, and troops in the Sherari cataract.

17th Feb. On the 17th, Colonel Butler, with the cavalry, occupied Salamat by 9 A.M., and at the same hour two companies of the Cornwalls landed on Sherri island. They found it deserted, and commenced to search for supplies. No cattle were found, but a considerable quantity of grain and dates, which, together with a supply of grain found on Uss island, completed the loads of our camel transport to its full carrying power.

The Sherari cataract caused great delay

SULEIMAN'S PROPERTY DESTROYED.

and considerable damage to boats. The Staffords and the Gordons each lost one boat, damaged beyond repair; but no lives were lost. By sunset the Cornwalls and three companies of the Gordons were in bivouac at Salamat, with the naval boat, Engineers, part of the field-hospital, and the cavalry. Headquarters also moved to Salamat, and occupied a house in a walled garden near the river-bank, belonging to a sister of Abu Bekr—an aunt, therefore, of Suleiman Wad Gamr. All the camel troops and convoy advanced to a good camping-ground, with ample forage, at the head of Sherari. Colonel Butler reconnoitred as far as Jebel Asma, and ascended the mountain. He reported clear water for nine miles from Salamat, no trace of enemy, and signs of cultivation along the river-bank beyond Jebel Asma.

The infantry continued their slow progress through the rapids. The remainder of the Gordons and the Staffords bivouacked at Sherari, and the Black Watch at Shoar.

On the previous evening a telegram from the acting Chief of the Staff had arrived, dated 13th, giving projects for sending us up supplies by hired camels, and stating what supplies we might possibly find at Abu Hamed. It informed me that a convoy was to start from Korosko on the 15th, which should reach Abu Hamed by the 20th or 21st; that Lord Wolseley anticipated that I could be ready to leave Abu Hamed on the 22d or 23d; but as he could not let me leave it until he should hear from General Buller, I was to await orders there, and he scarcely hoped I should reach Berber until the 13th or 14th March.

The telegram informed me of Lord Wolseley's proposals for the disposition of the troops after the projected capture of Berber, and of my own share, and that of my column, in these arrangements; but as subsequent events made these proposals void, it is not necessary to reproduce them here.

Captain Kekewich, D.A.A.G., also arrived with despatches, having left Korti on the

13th, and travelled through by camel in three days from Abu Dom. He brought me a letter from Lord Wolseley, and a copy of the instructions to General Buller, dated 12th February. With him returned from Abu Dom all the camel-corps men hitherto employed in carrying messages to and from that place,—arrangements having now been made with the commandant at Abu Dom, and the Vakeel at Birti, to supply messengers between these places, and with the latter to supply messengers from Birti to our camp. From Captain Kekewich we learned something of the situation on the desert side, so far as it was known at Korti up to the date of his leaving.

I replied to-day to the Chief of the Staff's telegram. I said frankly that I had no faith in the promises of any sheikhs that they would forward supplies to our camp, and that the convoy I was to receive at Abu Hamed from Korosko would enable my force to live till the 23d April, and no longer. I entered into questions of supply as affecting Lord Wolseley's proposed plan of operations, expressed my fears as to too sanguine an estimate having been formed both as to time and supplies, and again repeated that I could fix no dates, rate of progress being dependent on unknown conditions. I informed him that my rear battalion could only reach Salamat on the 19th.

Immediately on arrival at Salamat, Suleiman Wad Gamr's house had been taken possession of and searched. Many relics of the murder were found there, including one of poor Stewart's visiting-cards stained with blood, extracts from M. Herbin's papers, and photographs of M. Herbin and of the Austrian consul, presented by them to Mr Power. Chests of papers were found here, and great numbers of papers, with some few relics of the murder, on Sherri island. All these were secured and carefully examined by the interpreters; and orders were issued for all the troops at Salamat, except the pickets and a search-party ordered to Sherri island, to parade under the intelli-

SULEIMAN'S PROPERTY DESTROYED. 205

gence officers with axes, picks, and shovels, for the destruction of property. The other troops were ordered to close up to Salamat.

On the 18th the Gordons and Staffords 18th Feb. closed up on the Cornwalls at Salamat. The damaged boats of the Cornwalls and Gordons were repaired, the repairing party working till late. The Black Watch entered, and a portion passed through, the Sherari cataract.

The foraging party on Sherri island was successful, and brought over some forty camel-loads of grain in their boats. The troops were, I fear, much disappointed at not obtaining permission to destroy the houses and *sakyehs* on the island; but knowing that sooner or later we should have to return down the river, I forbade all destruction which, without any marked object to be gained, would interfere with the sources of supply on our return. The discipline of the troops was admirable. At one time some unauthorised burning of huts had taken place—not, I believe, by enlisted soldiers.

I had therefore published an order absolutely forbidding such irregularities, directing that any soldier, voyageur, or interpreter, plundering or setting fire to any house, *sakyeh*, or trees, without authority, was to be tried by summary court-martial, and pointing out that the offence was punishable with death. From that date the offence entirely ceased.

The troops had set to with a will to destroy Suleiman Wad Gamr's property. His house was a large one, standing on an eminence, with a colonnade supported by pillars, and several courtyards, each with several rooms. Roofs were pulled down, all wood available for firewood carried off, the walls shaken by charges of gun-cotton, and then utterly destroyed by the pick and the shovel. Beams and solid wooden doors, rare articles in this country, were destroyed by fire, and the house was razed to the ground. All his *sakyehs* were burnt, and his palm-trees were cut down and destroyed with fire.

By way of instruction, I ordered a wing of the Staffords to occupy Sheikh Omar's house as their bivouac this evening, and to place it in a defensible state, with orders to destroy it and the rest of Omar's property in the morning—Omar having escaped from the Vakeel, and rejoined Suleiman. Abu Bekr's property and that of his sister were spared.

These houses were of a higher class than any we had met with in the Shagiyeh or Monassir country. They had some attempt at ornament, and stood in gardens. In Abu Bekr's garden there was an orange-tree full of blossom, the only one we had seen since leaving Dongola.

Colvile's soldier-servant came into camp to-day, having had a curious adventure. He and a native servant of Colvile's, a Dongolese or Shagiyeh—I forget which—having left the bivouac of the previous day on camels with Colvile's baggage for Salamat, had taken a wrong turn in a wady, and had strayed into the desert, where they lost themselves and wandered about till nightfall, without water, and with little food. In the early morning they started to try and find the camp, and came upon a party of natives—doubtless nomad Monassir—tending cattle in a wady, with their women and children. The native servant asserted that they invited him to join them in killing the white man, but he told them there were 50,000 English at Salamat, who had come here on purpose to avenge another Englishman's death, and they would certainly all be killed if they hurt this one. At all events the two servants were shown their way to Salamat, and allowed to proceed unharmed, —another tolerably convincing proof of the moral effect of the fight at Kirbekan.

Butler reconnoitred four or five miles beyond Jebel Asma, reported the river clear, the country fairly open, and ample cultivation for foraging herds of animals. Orders were therefore issued for the advance to recommence in the morning, the Cornwalls leading, followed by the Gordons; the

SULEIMAN'S PROPERTY DESTROYED.

Staffords to halt at Salamat, repair their boats, and demolish Sheikh Omar's property. The Black Watch, battery, and convoy, to close up to Salamat. The cavalry to cover the advance with half the camel corps and two guns.

Reporting the intended advance to the Chief of the Staff to-day, I said: "I am unwilling to send back soldiers with messages, and native runners are limited in number. I shall therefore not attempt to communicate with you again after this, unless something special occurs, until I reach Abu Hamed, which I hope to do about 26th instant."

A native taken prisoner by our scouts stated he had left Abu Hamed four days ago, and had met crowds of men, women, and children, with cattle and camels, making their way up the river on both banks. He said they had few rifles, but many spears; and he had heard that Suleiman Wad Gamr was retiring on Berber, by order of Mohammed el Kheir. All the Monassir villages were deserted, but the Robatab villages were still inhabited.

19th Feb. On the 19th the advance from Salamat commenced. Omar's house was razed to the ground, and his *sakyehs* and palm-trees destroyed. A quantity of grain was collected. The cavalry and camel troops started with grain for six days; every transport camel was fully loaded up, and the camels had a good feed. The last of the troops and the convoy closed up at Salamat, and were ordered to advance on the following day.

CHAPTER XII.

HEBBEH—THE PASSAGE OF THE NILE.

On the 19th, Colonel Butler on the bank, 19th Feb. and Colonel Alleyne in his boat, reconnoitred for a distance of between eleven and twelve miles from Salamat, and Butler selected a site for a bivouac at Sulimanyeh, about nine miles above Salamat, and about two and a half miles below the wreck of Stewart's steamer; and the Cornwalls, Gordons, and details concentrated there by five o'clock. Butler reported that when he arrived opposite the wreck, two Arab scouts on camels began to shout from the right bank, and then rode off to the north. We had seen the enemy's scouts in the same way on our arrival at Salamat. A prisoner taken beyond the site of the wreck asserted that Suleiman Wad Gamr had arrived at Suliman-yeh on the 16th, and had gone northwards on the 17th, taking with him Fakri Wad Etman; he was said to be accompanied by about 400 men and a number of women and children, with many cattle, camels, donkeys, and much baggage. Lekalik, with the force which had retreated from the Shukook pass, was said to have preceded Suleiman Wad Gamr, two of the sheikhs that had been with him at the Shukook having been sent direct to Berber.

Another prisoner informed us that he had left the neighbourhood of Abu Hamed on the 14th. He heard that many men from Berber had arrived there, and that there were 2000 Ababdehs, 1000 Bisharin, and some Robatab assembled there to defend Abu Hamed.

Although the accounts of prisoners were by no means to be trusted, there was a persistency in the accounts of the flights along the left bank which, coupled with the hasty and complete abandonment of the Shukook pass, led me to believe that the enemy in front of us was in a state of demoralisation, and unlikely to make any stand. On the other hand, the presence of the enemy's mounted scouts on the right bank—their defiant attitude as they retired, menacing us by voice and gesture, as the enemy's outposts on the left bank had menaced us before Kirbekan, but at no other time—led me to believe the consistent reports that on the right bank at, or possibly before reaching, Abu Hamed, we should meet with a more determined opposition, in which it was probable the news of the fall of Khartoum might induce both Ababdeh and Bisharin Arabs to join.

I was therefore anxious to cross my mounted troops and transport animals over to the right bank as soon as practicable, and resolved to do this at the first convenient locality. Little was to be gained by advancing farther on the left bank; for though there was perhaps more cultivation on it than on the right bank, both were barren sandy wastes, with only occasional patches of growing crops; and as at Sulimanyeh we were within little more than forty miles of Abu Hamed, and all accounts united in agreeing that there was but one more rapid of any importance—that close to Mograt island—the time before reaching Abu Hamed should now be so brief, that a little better grazing for the camels did not weigh against the importance of effecting the crossing without opposition.

I had attached Colonel Colvile to the advanced guard under Butler since his arrival in camp after guiding the convoy through the Shukook, with instructions to send in a sketch daily to accompany Colonel Butler's report. Judging from his sketch received this evening at Salamat that a favourable crossing-place would be found near Sulimanyeh, I wrote to Colonel Butler saying that the whole of the troops at Salamat would move to Sulimanyeh on the 20th, that I should myself start at 7 and be in his camp at 8.30, and that I begged him to wait for me there. He was to send on the Cornwalls and Gordons in the morning by river, but not the guns or any baggage or baggage-animals till after my arrival; and two companies of each of the leading battalions were to halt on the left bank opposite to Hebbeh, with all the axes, picks, and shovels the battalions could furnish. No troops were to be allowed to land on the right bank. My intention was, if there was a favourable crossing-place at Sulimanyeh, to cross all the animals and guns over there with the boats of the two rear battalions, to visit and examine the site of Stewart's murder, and then destroy the house and surrounding property of Fakri Wad Etman. If there should not be a favourable crossing-place, the dispositions were such that no delay whatever would be caused.

On the morning of the 20th I reached Sulimanyeh at the hour named, and told Colonel Butler my views. He said that

20th Feb.

Hebbeh itself afforded so favourable a site for the crossing, that he had directed Alleyne to halt all the boats there, pending my decision. On arrival opposite Hebbeh, directly opposite the wrecked steamer, I found all the conditions for a favourable crossing fulfilled. On this side a high commanding bank, with clear view over the neighbouring country, affording an excellent position for infantry and guns both to sweep the opposite bank and hold their own against any attack from this side. Below the high bank, but easily approached by a natural ramp, a long sandbank sloping gradually into the water. On the opposite side, but a quarter of a mile below, a high Nile island, forming a strong position for infantry, and with a similar sandbank—the breadth from the left bank to the high Nile island being about 300 yards. The high Nile island itself was separated from the right bank only by a narrow channel, over which at one place there was a dry crossing.

I at once ordered the crossing to be

undertaken. Sending the Cornwalls over in their boats to establish themselves on the high Nile island, and to take up a position to cover the crossing, and bringing half the Gordons to the high ground on the left bank, where I directed them to form a zareeba, I sent back orders to Sulimanyeh for the guns and baggage there to be brought on by their escort, and for the whole of the troops and convoy on their arrival there, both by land and water, to be pushed on to Hebbeh.

We could see with our glasses that we were being watched from behind the sand-hills less than a mile out in the desert on the right bank, and Butler at once crossed over with a scouting-party of Hussars, before whom the enemy's scouts retired. About 11 A.M. the baggage of the advanced guard and two guns arrived from Sulimanyeh, and the guns were at once placed in position. Our Hussars formed a line of vedettes on a radius of a mile and a half from the point of crossing on the left bank, and those first sent across placed vedettes in commanding positions about a mile out on the right bank. About the same hour, 11 A.M., the leading boats of the Black Watch and Staffords arrived. They had advanced along both banks from Salamat. By one o'clock the remainder of the battery and the convoy arrived, under escort of half the camel corps.

The troops and baggage were crossed over in the following order:—

Scouting-party 19th Hussars.

Support, consisting of half the camel corps.

Two guns of the Egyptian battery, with their camels—having been replaced in their position on the left bank by the four remaining guns on their arrival; they were placed in position on high Nile island as soon as crossed over.

Cavalry baggage.

Camel corps baggage.

Remainder of the 19th Hussars—having been relieved on vedette duty by the half of the camel corps which had escorted the convoy.

Camels of the four guns on the left bank.

Headquarter baggage and horses, and infantry regimental horses.

The transport company, camels, and loads.

The cattle and donkeys.

The four guns.

Remaining half of the camel corps.

Each animal was towed over by a boat, —its saddle, load, and driver or rider being, as a rule, ferried across in that boat. The ferrying commenced at 11 A.M. and ended for the day at 5.30 P.M., recommenced at 7 A.M. and finished at 2 P.M., having thus occupied thirteen and a half hours of actual work, during which time 780 animals, with their equipment and loads, and their drivers or riders, and six guns, had been taken across.

20th to 21st Feb.

The crossing was effected under the superintendence of Colonel Alleyne, assisted by all the staff officers available. Two crossing-places were worked at the same time; and it was found that as many as fifty boats could be simultaneously employed, but not more. The crossing was made down-stream, the actual distance traversed being about 400 yards.

The water being too shallow for the boats to come quite up to the dry shore of the sandbank, each animal, having had a rope fastened securely round its head by one of Lieutenant Bourke's blue-jackets, or by one of the Egyptian camel-men, was led into the water, and the loose end of the rope was handed to a man in the stern. The boat was then rowed off from shore, and the animal followed till out of its depth, when it commenced to swim, or, in some cases of camels, lay on its side and allowed itself to be towed across. The horses swam freely; and it was found important to let them have ample length of rope, with their heads freed from any strain. With the camels, on the other hand, it was found necessary to have a very short rope, and to hold the animal's head well above water, close up to the boat. The camel is an indifferent swimmer. He can make his way down-stream for a short time, but soon becomes exhausted; and he cannot swim against a strong stream. The tendency always is for his head to go under, and his hindquarters to rise above the water; and the Egyptian artillerymen counteracted this by sitting astride on the rumps of their camels, thus forcing the quarters down, when the heads correspondingly rise. The camels which were least exhausted were those that lay on their sides, and, with their heads held well up close to the hands of the man in the stern, allowed themselves, thus suspended, to be towed across without attempting to swim.

The veterinary surgeon with his assistants was stationed on the right bank, and administered restoratives to any animals which appeared exhausted on arrival. I have noticed, for future guidance, that the points chiefly to be attended to, in addition to the length of rope above-mentioned, are the tying of the head-rope, great care being necessary to prevent its slipping or getting round the animal's nostrils; the hours of crossing, which should not be very early or very late, but when the sun is well up, so that there is less risk of chill; the pace of the boats, which, in the case of horses and camels, should be regulated by their pace of swimming; immediate administration of restoratives to exhausted animals; and gentle exercise after crossing for all.

We lost only three camels. One, the rope having broken, floated down the rapid water and was drowned. Two died from suffocation, the rope having slipped and closed their nostrils. Six others, nearly all from among those which crossed over late in the evening, suffered subsequently from epileptic fits, similar to staggers in a horse.

Of these, three recovered, and the rest died; though had they been able to rest for a few days, they also would in all probability have recovered. No casualty occurred among the horses or cattle. One donkey died of exhaustion.

CHAPTER XIII.

HEBBEH—THE SCENE OF COLONEL STEWART'S MURDER.

20th to 21st Feb. WHILE the crossing was in progress on the 20th, I visited the wreck and the scene of the murder, taking with me those of the staff who could be spared, and the commanding officers of regiments. We found the steamer impaled on a large rock, about two hundred yards from the proper right bank of the river. She was a much larger vessel than we had supposed her to be. She was seventy feet in length from stem to stern, and twenty-two feet in breadth over her paddles: the depth of her hold was four feet six inches. Plates of iron a quarter of an inch thick protected her sides, pitted with bullet-marks, and torn through in places by case-shot or splinters of shell. She lay with her keel sixteen feet above the present level of the water, in a channel studded with rocks—an intricate narrow labyrinth; while on the left bank of the river there was open clear water for nearly three hundred yards in breadth, so that at the time of the wreck there must have been nearly four hundred yards of open water on that bank. Yet her pilot had steered her into this rocky maze, where, even at high Nile, many of the rocks must have shown above water. To us it seemed incredible that the wreck was an accident, for it was almost impossible to believe she had not been purposely steered to her destruction. And yet, who can say? At high Nile she would have come rushing down the swift water above, and a very small error in steering would have caused her to be swept in here.

The natives had stripped her of everything that could be of use, leaving her a mere shell. All her wood-work had been carried away, including the floats of her paddles, and such iron as was sufficiently portable. The after-part of her hold was filled with sand, her bows were high out of water. A few torn scraps of letters and paper, of no particular interest, were littered about; but there was nothing whatever worth preserving as a relic.

From the steamer we walked by a dry causeway to the mainland—right bank—which we followed down-stream for about four hundred yards, when we came to the first group of houses of Hebbeh. We had brought with us Abu Bekr, the uncle of Suleiman Wad Gamr, and I have seldom seen a man in a more wholesome state of fear. He evidently thought that we had brought him here to execute him on the spot. But he mastered his terrors, and pointed out to us the house of Fakri Wad Etman. It was an ordinary native mud-house, the external entrance being into a small courtyard, on one side of which was the house. But it was not here, Abu Bekr told us, that the strangers would have been received. In this house the women lived, and no strangers would have been admitted there. The murder must have taken place in the *salaamlik*, or guest-chamber—a detached mud-hut of one room only, some fifty yards from the dwelling-house. We entered this small room, stooping to pass under the low doorway with feelings of awe. But there was nothing to remind us of the terrible tragedy that had taken place there six months before. There were no signs of blood. The floor and all the ground round the hut had been carefully strewn with fine sand.

A hundred yards in front of the door, on the river-bank, stood a group of palms, the scene of another tragedy. But I will let the story be told in the words of one who was fortunate enough to escape from the scene, as taken down from his own lips by Major Slade, through the medium of an interpreter, on the 1st February.

STATEMENT OF HASSEIN ISMAIN.

"I am the stoker of the steamer Abbas, which left Khartoum about six months ago, on a Wednesday. Stewart Pasha, two European consuls, twelve Greeks, five artillery soldiers, four Arab women and four slave women, and seven native crew, were on board. The captain of the steamer was Mahomed Saf. Eddin, and the *reises* [pilots] Ali Bishteeli and Mohamed. Two other steamers accompanied us to beyond Berber, and four nuggers sailed with us, which were towed as far as Berber by the two steamers. The steamers shelled the forts at Berber, and when our steamer was safely past, they left us, and we continued our journey with the four nuggers. We left the nuggers behind us, just before reaching Abu Hamed, and steamed on.

"On a Thursday, three days before the end of the month of Dhul-kadeh [18th September], at about nine in the morning, the steamer ran on a rock about two feet below the surface in Wad Gamr's country. Before we struck we had seen several people running away into the hills on both banks. When we struck, the small boat was filled with our things, and everything was landed on the small island. Four trips were made between the steamer and the island, and when everything of value had been landed,

Stewart Pasha returned to the steamer himself, drove a nail into the vent of the gun, and filed the projecting part off. The gun was bolted to the deck of the ship, and the artillery soldiers set it free, and threw it overboard. Two boxes of gun-ammunition were also thrown overboard at the same time.

"While this was going on, several people came to the right bank and shouted out, 'Give us peace and grace.' Hassan Bey, belonging to the Telegraph Department, acted as interpreter to Stewart Pasha, and told the natives that they would have peace. Four or five natives swam over to the island, and Hassan Bey returned with them in the small boat to the right bank, and saw Sheikh Suleiman Wad Gamr, who was in a house near the bank. Hassan asked him for camels to take the party to Merawi, and Suleiman ordered four camels to be taken to the bank to be loaded with the baggage, and Hassan returned. Suleiman then sent two men to the island to invite Stewart Pasha to land and come to the house. Everybody then landed on the right bank, taking with them all the baggage. Hassan Bey then went to the house of a blind man named Etman Fakri, with two men; and he was told by Suleiman to ask Stewart Pasha and the two consuls to come in and drink coffee, and arrange about the price to be paid for the camels. This was at about

4 P. M. The soldiers wanted to accompany Stewart Pasha as a guard; but Hassan Bey said that it would frighten the people, and the camels would not be given.

"Stewart Pasha, the two consuls, and Hassan Bey then entered the house of Etman Fakri. They were all unarmed except Stewart Pasha, who had a small revolver on his belt. After a short time, I saw Suleiman come out of the house with a copper water-pot in his hand. He made a sign to the people who were standing about the village armed with swords and spears; and immediately the people divided into two parties, one going to the house of Etman Fakri, and the other rushing to the place (by the palms) where the rest of Stewart's party was assembled. I was with this party, and when the natives charged us, we threw ourselves into the river. The natives fired at us and killed many; others were drowned. I swam to a small island, and remained there till it was dark, when I swam to the left bank. I remained there for some time, and then made my way to Hamdab. There I was taken by a man called Taha Wad Fadeil, made prisoner, and taken to Sheikh Omar, uncle of Suleiman Wad Gamr, at Birti. He told me to remain with him and not escape, and he would treat me well. I have been at Birti ever since, and remained there after the dervishes ran away the day before yesterday.

SCENE OF COL. STEWART'S MURDER.

"I heard that when the natives entered the house of Etman Fakri, they fell upon Stewart Pasha and the consuls, and killed them all. Hassan Bey escaped, wounded in the arm by a knife, and went to Berber. When the natives rushed into the hut, Hassan Bey held the blind man in front of him, and thus was saved. The captain was killed.

"Two of the artillery soldiers, the two *reises*, and three of the native crew, are alive at Berber. Four full-grown slaves, one woman slave, and two young ones, are also alive, and were near Birti, in the desert looking after cattle, a month ago. The money found was divided amongst the natives who fell upon the party. Everything else was sent to Berber. Two bundles of spears, and two suits of chain-armour, the property of one of the consuls, were at Birti.

"All the bodies of those murdered were thrown into the river."

We found but few traces of the murder: some fragments of books, more of poor Stewart's visiting-cards, a shirt-sleeve stained with blood, and a few papers, apparently belonging to MM. Herbin and Power. At Sherari island we had found five pages of Stewart's diary, describing Gordon's entry into Abu Hamed and Berber on the way from Korosko to Khartoum.

We pressed Abu Bekr as to how Suleiman Wad Gamr came to be at the scene of the wreck, and he told us that as soon as the steamer went ashore, Fakri Wad Etman had sent a message to Suleiman Wad Gamr at Salamat; and that Suleiman had immediately ordered his camels, and had hastened to Hebbeh. This was quite consistent with the stoker's account of the wreck having taken place at nine, and Suleiman's first appearance on the scene some time in the afternoon, when Hassan Bey went to Fakri Wad Etman's house, after all the baggage had been removed from the steamer, the gun spiked, and the ammunition destroyed.

<small>21st Feb.</small> Orders were issued for the destruction of the property of Fakri Wad Etman and the village of Hebbeh on the 21st. The work was superintended by the officers of the Intelligence Department, who searched everywhere for papers or relics, boring and

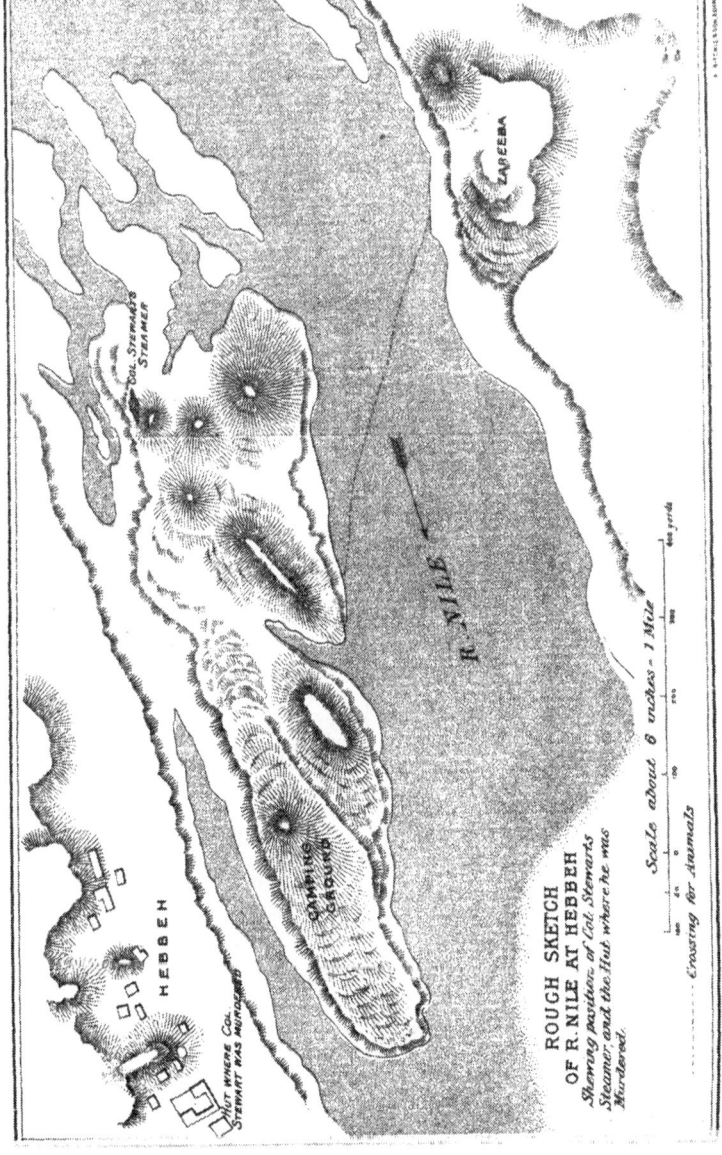

digging wherever the ground seemed disturbed. Some skeletons were found, but they were old, and of Africans. Little or nothing of interest was discovered. There was no trace of that journal of which Gordon spoke in such high terms. Fakri Wad Etman's houses were destroyed, his *sakyehs* burnt, and his palm-trees cut down and set on fire : his *salaamlik* was razed to the ground.

CHAPTER XIV.

HUELLA—THE END OF THE MONASSIR COUNTRY.

21st Feb. On the night of the 21st, headquarters bivouacked on the high Nile island with the Cornwalls and Staffords, mounted troops, and convoy. The Gordons and Black Watch bivouacked on the left bank. Butler reconnoitred a few miles to the front, and reported the river very swift for about two miles, and then again comparatively easy. With the exception of an occasional small village with cultivation, the open desert of yellow sand reached to the water's edge.

We now were about to leave the region of rocks, and to enter a country where there was breathing-space. The character of the opposition likely to be encountered was also changed. We had no longer to fear ambuscades in ravines, or to expect to find rocky gorges held against us by ensconced riflemen. If the enemy on the right bank meant battle before our reaching Abu Hamed, he must fight us in comparatively open ground, where the discipline of our troops, and the superiority of our weapons, must tell with deadly effect; and, if report was true, we might expect here to meet the nomad Bisharin Arabs, whose tactics would probably be like those of the Hadendowas at Teb and Tamai, or the enemy encountered by Herbert Stewart. The change was a great relief; but we had also to consider that the enemy we should now encounter would consist of fresh troops, undaunted by previous defeat.

The following orders were therefore issued: "In the further advance of the column by river, every effort must be made to keep the boats well closed up, not by constant delays on the part of the leading boats to wait for the remainder, but by strenuous exertions on the part of the crews of the boats in rear to keep up with those leading the advance. Commanding officers will impress upon all non-commissioned officers and men that the success of the expedition, and its safety while moving by river, depend mainly upon the amount of energy which they put into their work.

"The advance will be covered on the right bank by the mounted troops, who will give warning to the leading boats of any aggressive movement of the enemy. Should the officers commanding the mounted troops report the enemy advancing to attack, the leading boats will fall back on the rear boats of the leading half-battalion, and the rear half-battalion will close up. As soon as the leading half battalion is concentrated, the troops will be landed and at once formed up to meet the attack in the strongest available position. All following battalions, unless specially ordered to the contrary, will close up on the leading battalion, land, and await orders."

END OF THE MONASSIR COUNTRY.

The orders for an unexpected landing issued by Major-General Earle on 19th January were republished, and attention called to their salient points. The various departmental boats were assigned their places in the column.

"The advance by land of the guns and convoy, and their escort, must be guided by circumstances," ran the order, "which may change from day to day; therefore no precise rules can be laid down, but all transport must be kept well together, must move on as wide a front as the nature of the ground permits, and must invariably be protected by flankers, well thrown out into the desert."

On the morning of the 22d the column 22d Feb. advanced, the Gordon Highlanders leading, at 6.45 A.M. The river immediately above our crossing-place was very swift and difficult, and it was late in the afternoon before the last boat was through it. Two miles of swift and rocky water followed. The two leading battalions and mounted troops—

under Colonel Butler — bivouacked at a small village about six miles above Hebbeh, and nearly opposite a remarkable rock of white marble, standing alone in the river, called Hajar el Baida, "the white rock." The cavalry reconnoitred six miles to the front, and saw no trace of the enemy.

The remainder of the column bivouacked at El Kab, about a mile below Hajar el Baida. Here there was a small village with a fair quantity of growing crops. There was also a large stone fort on a high rock over the river, and another on the opposite bank, of precisely the same nature as those already spoken of at Kabenat, below Birti. We took up a strong defensive position here, with a company on outpost on a high detached rock in front, only accessible by one steep path. The country beyond was flat desert, or undulating sand-dunes.

Before moving off from Hebbeh in the morning, I had released a spy of El Zain. This man had been brought in by our scouts, and after telling many different stories, had at last confessed to being a spy of El Zain, sent by him to obtain information of our strength and movements. I suppose he ought to have been hanged, but I thought he would be more useful alive; and having extracted from him such information as he would give as to El Zain's position and strength, I let him see the whole force, and then sent him back to El Zain, bidding him tell that robber-chief what he had seen at Kirbekan and Hebbeh.

On the 23d the boats advanced simultaneously from both camps, moving in parallel columns by both banks. Much swift water was encountered, but no rapid necessitating tracking. By an early hour in the afternoon the leading boats had reached a cluster of grass huts at the head of a swift rapid, said by Abu Bekr to be named Huella, and to be the last habitations in the Monassir country.

23d Feb.

Before nightfall, by dint of great exertion, the last boat of the column had closed up, and our 215 boats lay moored side by side along the bank, having averaged 10½ miles rowing against very swift water.

The mounted troops having reconnoitred five miles to the front, reported good clear water, and having seen no enemy, though traces of their camel scouts, fell back to Huella.

The convoy and artillery, marching on a broad front over the undulating desert sand, also closed up. On the way I had halted them, and told Major Wodehouse, who commanded the convoy throughout, to make dispositions to resist an attack from the left front. The camels were rapidly parked, and a strong front of fire brought to bear; and I was satisfied that the convoy, which was moving with wide-flanking scouts, would run no risk of being taken at a disadvantage. The convoy then moved on to Huella.

Village Huella was not, in any sense of the term, and there was no cultivation. It was apparently only the temporary resting-place of nomad Arabs, who brought flocks and herds there to water and graze. There was no forage for camels, but we were assured that the following day's advance through easy water would bring us to cultivation in the Robatab country. The camels had brought loads of cut forage with them from El Kab and Hajar el Baida, and an issue of grain was sanctioned.

Shortly after leaving El Kab, we had been hailed by a camel-man on the left bank, and having ferried him across, ascertained that he was a spy sent from the Intelligence Department at headquarters, who had been sent to Berber with orders to report his news to us on his way back. It differed in little from what we previously knew. He brought back with him a messenger whom we had sent from Hebbeh on the 21st with despatches. This messenger had been seized by some dervishes in the Shukook pass, his papers had been taken from him, and he had been stripped. The dervishes were proceeding to kill him, when the camel-man from Berber appeared on the scene, and they fled hastily.

In the evening, a boy whom we had sent with instructions to try and reach Abu Hamed, and bring back news, returned, saying that he had been stopped by a party of dervishes on the right bank about ten miles from our camp, and made prisoner, but had escaped. He had gathered from them that there were only a few of the enemy between us and Abu Hamed on this bank, but that the Monassir and Robatab, and a force from Berber with Suleiman Wad Gamr and other sheikhs, were holding a rocky position on the other bank, at a place called Shamkiyeh, near Jebel Gergerib, and intended to oppose our advance there. They were not aware of our having crossed all our mounted troops to the right bank.

We bivouacked in a strong semicircular position on the yellow sand, covering our boats and mounted troops on the sandbank below. At nine o'clock, being now within the distance, we fired a rocket from the nearest high hill, and another five minutes later—a preconcerted signal to inform Rundle's scouts, who should be on the watch, that we were within thirty miles of Abu Hamed. I walked round the position, and saw that perfect order reigning which came from the constant repetition and constant supervision of the nightly bivouac in readiness to meet instantaneous attack. Troops peacefully sleeping, tired with the hard day's work, beside their piled arms; double sentries alert and motionless, watching with trained eyes every foot of the open space before the bivouac; officers on watch vigilant; perfect silence everywhere. Not once, in any camp I had been in, had there ever been a sign of a false alarm. This day's work had been the best ever performed by the troops. Two hundred and fifteen boats had been rowed by their strong arms through ten or eleven miles of the swiftest water possible to contend with. Our wounded were all doing well. No death had occurred among them since we left our camp at Dulka. The physical condition of the men was magnificent. We had completed a month out from Hamdab—a month of almost unparalleled exertion, passed entirely in the open air. We had not sent back one sick man; we had had but one death from disease; and the total sick-list of the force was now only eighteen, a proportion of 6.4 per 1000—a condition of health which I believe to be unprecedented among any troops in any campaign. The men were in high spirits; and there were two battalions, neither of which had yet been in action, longing for the chance of emulating those who had fought so gallantly at Kirbekan. It was the first time I had seen the whole force in one bivouac; and I lay down with a feeling of perfect confidence in their power to conquer any host of Arabs that the Mahdi could bring against them from the farthest corners of the Soudan.

In four days, I said to myself, we shall be at Abu Hamed. We shall open up the Korosko desert-route, and our doing so will ring through the Soudan, and weaken the knees of the followers of Mahomet Achmet.

CHAPTER XV.

RECALL—BACK TO SALAMAT.

24th Feb. I HAD issued orders that to give the men more rest after so good a day's work, *réveillé* would not sound till half-past five; and it was seven o'clock on the morning of the 24th before the first boat was in readiness to move. Some letters and Reuter's telegrams had arrived the night before by camel-post; and an opportunity thus occurring of sending back to Korti, I reported in the most cheerful terms to Lord Wolseley. Seeking for something in my despatch-box, I came across the following cutting which I had taken at Halfa from the 'Army and Navy Gazette' of the 13th September 1884 :—

"The opinions which were expressed in this

BACK TO SALAMAT. 247

journal as soon as the orders were made known for the construction of those ridiculous row-boats for the expedition on the Nile have been corroborated by the assent and concurrence of every man who has any experience of the country and the river. A more wicked waste of money was never perpetrated, a more silly quackery was never devised, by any public department than that of which Lord Hartington and the Duke of Cambridge, representing the War Office and the Horse Guards, have really and truly been guilty in ordering that monstrous armada of boats, that unfloatable flotilla for the Nile! Burn them for firewood! Send them to Jericho, to ply on the Palestine canal of the future! Make matches of them — do anything with them! Put men in them, and try to send them up the Nile cataracts —never, we beg of you!"

Well, there they lay, 215 boats of the unfloatable flotilla, floating above all the worst cataracts of the Nile, within ten miles of the last of that series of rapids of which it was said in every map published before the expedition started, "Between Gerendid and Mograt cataracts (140 miles), the river is unnagivable at low Nile." Said, and truly said hitherto. It had been left for British soldiers and British "ridiculous row-boats" to navigate the unnavigable, and to convey an army of 3000 men, with their stores and munitions of war, to within twenty-six miles of Abu Hamed.

Our cavalry scouts and patrols had long been out. The leading boats of the Gordons had just pushed off. The main body of the cavalry had moved out of camp. Colonel Butler was riding past my bivouac, when a messenger arrived with a despatch from Korti. I opened it. It was mostly in cipher; but some words in clear caught my eye, sent a cold shiver through me, and caused me at once to sound the halt.

This is what the message said when it had been deciphered:—

"KORTI, *20th February.*

"Buller evacuated Gubat. His main body went to Gakdul with all sick and wounded. He remains with about 1500 men at Abu Klea. The enemy have now begun to fire into his camp there, and have killed and wounded some of his men. He awaits camels to fall back on Gakdul,

BACK TO SALAMAT. 249

which I hope he will begin to do to-morrow, the 21st instant; but owing to the weak state of his camels, all his men must go on foot. I have abandoned all hope of going to Berber before the autumn campaign begins. You will therefore not go to Abu Hamed, but having burned and destroyed everything in the neighbourhood where Stewart was murdered, you will withdraw all your force to Abu Dom, near Merawi, bringing all the Mudir's troops with you.

"Please express to the troops Lord Wolseley's high appreciation of their gallant conduct in action, and of the military spirit they have displayed in overcoming the great difficulties presented by the river. Having punished the Monassir people for Stewart's murder, it is not intended to undertake any further military operations until after the approaching hot season.

"Further orders will be sent to you upon your reaching Abu Dom. Until you have occupied the Shukook pass, and made sure of every one through it, you had better keep this telegram entirely to yourself and Butler. Of course, if you are in the presence of the enemy when you receive this, you must defeat him before turning back. If you do not receive this before you have reached Abu Hamed, or are so near to it that it is merely a question of occupying it without opposition, you must halt there, and send back information at once to me, when I will start the convoy from Korosko, which I do not otherwise mean to despatch. Of course it is impossible at this distance to give you positive orders, but Lord Wolseley has every confidence in your military discretion."

But little time was needed for decision. The cup was snatched from our lips, but we must bear the disappointment bravely. The conditions in which I found myself gave no reasonable excuse for pressing on. And lightly as the message touched upon General Buller's difficulties, there was sufficient in it to give cause for anxiety as to the result of his retreat. That he had not retired one hour before it was necessary to do so was a certainty. If his troops should be surrounded by vast numbers of the late besiegers of Khartoum, who had already had three weeks within which to collect to oppose him, his situation might be full of peril. I knew Lord Wolseley could have but a handful of men at Korti, and the flower of his force was here in the River

Column. I had but one course open to me —to make my way to Abu Dom with all possible speed. I showed the telegram to Colonel Butler. He entirely agreed with me, and I sent back the following reply:—

"I received your telegram this morning, just as the troops were starting up river. I am, by the map, about twenty-six miles from Abu Hamed. I am not in the immediate presence of the enemy, nor have the patrols, who have been six miles beyond this, had any touch of the enemy. Nor do I anticipate meeting the enemy to-day, should I continue my advance. My latest information is that the enemy intend to fight at Abu Hamed, and I anticipate opposition if I advance upon it. There is a cataract between me and Abu Hamed, and if opposed, it might take some days before I could occupy the place. I am confident I could beat any force opposed to me, but I feel it my duty, in view of the facts contained in the first part of your telegram, to fall back immediately to Abu Dom, and I shall fall back to Hebbeh to-day. I shall return by the right bank."

By returning along the right bank to Merawi, I should avoid all danger of opposition to the convoy in the Shukook pass, where a few men could cause serious delay. It was evidently impossible for any serious opposition to be organised at very short notice on the right bank.

I then issued the following orders to the troops: "The Brigadier-General announces to the troops that since they entered the boats this morning he has received a telegram from Lord Wolseley, stating that, after the Monassir tribe has been punished for Colonel Stewart's murder, it is not intended to undertake any further military operations until after the approaching hot season. The furthest limits of the Monassir country having been reached, and the punishment for Colonel Stewart's murder having been, so far as possible, inflicted, the troops will now return through the Monassir country to Birti. The column will therefore move upon Hebbeh to-day." Lord Wolseley's expression of appreciation was also published, and the following was added: "The Brigadier-General has to remind the troops that the descent of this swift river will require even greater care than its ascent. All will depend upon the vigilance of the men in the bows, and the coolness and resource of the men steering."

The following instructions for the information of officers in charge of boats descending the Nile were drawn up by Lieut.-Colonel Alleyne :—

" 1. Owing to the swiftness of the stream, the boats will move over it at a rapid rate, consequently if a boat strikes a rock she will probably receive a severe injury. Accidents of this nature can be avoided, *first*, by the vigilance of the poleman, who should sound frequently ; *secondly*, by not allowing boats to close up or crowd upon each other when descending a rapid.

" 2. As a rule, when descending a rapid the crew must row, otherwise the boat will not steer.

" 3. The last two (2) boats of each battalion should be nearly empty, so that in the event of a boat being severely injured in a rapid, they may be able to take in her cargo or return to her assistance. All other boats should have equal draught of water.

" 4. Coxwains must follow the lead given by boats with pilots in them.

"5. After descending a rapid, the leading boats must halt until the rear boats join them.

"In difficult rapids special arrangements will be made for taking each boat through with Canadian pilots."

While halted, I was informed that a number of men on camels had been seen in the desert to the south-west. Patrols were sent out, but the camels turned out to be only the product of a fevered imagination. However, some delay had been caused; and so the men were ordered to dine early, and then move down-stream. The mounted troops were ordered to patrol up-stream and cover the retirement by a forward reconnaissance, while the convoy with an escort returned towards Hebbeh. At noon the boats commenced to move downstream, led by Colonel Denison commanding the Canadian voyageurs. The column moved in reversed order from its progress up-stream. The Staffords led, followed successively by the Black Watch and Cornwalls. The Gordons brought up the rear.

The three leading battalions reached Hebbeh, and bivouacked on the high Nile island. The Gordons were halted with the convoy, camel battery, and part of the camel corps at Umsyal, a village three miles above Hebbeh, where there was plenty of good forage, with orders to destroy houses and *sakyehs* before leaving. The cavalry and the remainder of the camel corps having patrolled to within sight of the island of Mograt and seen no enemy, halted at El Kab, under Colonel Butler.

The casualties amongst the boats were three damaged and repaired, and one total wreck. The horses and camels had suffered heavily from the heat, and the heavy sand fetlock-deep. Four camels and one horse died of exhaustion. I therefore ordered a halt for the next day, except that all the troops and convoy were to close up to Hebbeh.

The evening brought a messenger with despatches, all of earlier date than that received in the morning, and not containing orders of recall; also messages from the Commandant at Abu Dom and the Vakeel, to say that neither for love nor money could they get any more messengers to come to us. It did not matter now; we were going to them. But I have often since thought, that if that messenger had not been so pressing who reached us with the order of recall, we should have been in presence of the enemy; we should have had another fight, and as we had twice as many troops present as at Kirbekan, probably an even more telling victory. I must then have occupied Abu Hamed; and the fact of our doing so would, I believe, have materially improved our position in the Soudan. But fate willed it otherwise.

25th Feb. On the 25th the troops were employed in completing the destruction of the houses and *sakyehs* of the village of Hebbeh, and on the island of El Kun, and the Gordons and mounted troops closed up on the column.

A detachment of Hussars and camel

corps was sent to a village about three miles down-stream, with orders to march off at the same hour as the boats in the morning. Supplies were equalised among the regiments, in proportion to their number of boats, and ordered to be so divided as to bring all boats to as nearly as possible the same draught of water.

Orders were issued to the following effect: The Gordons were to move off at 7.45 A.M., followed at successive intervals of three-quarters of an hour by the Staffords, Black Watch, and Cornwalls—the last regiment furnishing the rear-guard. In every battalion except the rear battalion, the officer second in command was to bring up the rear of his battalion, being held responsible for bringing on all boats of his own battalion, and all boats of details moving with his battalion or between it and the preceding battalion. He was not to move on himself until every one of these boats that could be brought on had preceded him. Each battalion, as previously ordered, was to have two empty boats moving in rear of the others.

The officer commanding the rear battalion was himself to bring up the rear of the whole column. He was to tell off four companies of his battalion as a rear-guard, and to move with this rear-guard in rear of all boats not abandoned, being held responsible that no boat of the column was left behind unless necessarily abandoned, and that all abandoned boats were destroyed. On arrival in camp he was to report verbally to headquarters that every boat had arrived.

Major Flood, 12th Hussars, was to cover the rear of the column with the mounted troops; and the command of the rear-guard on shore and on the river was given to Colonel Butler, to whom the officer commanding the rear battalion was to report, should he be unable to reach headquarters camp.

The number of repairing boats was increased to four,—one to move in rear of

BACK TO SALAMAT. 259

each battalion, and assist in repairing any boats that might be damaged, and could not be repaired regimentally.

In reporting to Lord Wolseley in the evening, I said that, after consultation with Butler and Alleyne, I was of opinion it would take six or seven days to Birti, and six or seven from that place to Merawi. My place of crossing would depend on the information I might receive at Birti.

On the morning of the 26th the troops moved as ordered. By noon the advanced guard of mounted troops and the convoy, with two battalions of infantry, were concentrated at Amarim, opposite Salamat, on the right bank, near the head of Sherri island. We on the bank rode along a flat wady at some distance from the bank the greater part of the way. On reaching Amarim, I at once rode on with Alleyne and Peel to inspect the channel between the right bank and Sherri island. We found it impracticable for boats from its shallowness, and the distance of the right bank

26th Feb.

from the left bank of the river increased rapidly, it being evident that very large islands lay between.

I was satisfied that it would be now practically impossible to combine with accuracy the movements of the mounted troops and of the boats. We were now about to commence the descent of the formidable series of cataracts between Salamat and Ooli; and I decided that my own proper place was with the boats, and that the command of the mounted troops and convoy should be confided to Colonel Butler. Moving a cavalry advanced guard about three miles down-stream, and leaving the remainder at Amarim, where I halted the Cornwalls on their arrival for the purpose of completing the mounted troops up to six days' rations from the boats, I instructed Colonel Butler to advance at 7 A.M. on the 27th, sending the Cornwalls by river at the same hour. He was to endeavour to keep touch of the troops in boats, but failing that, to make his way to Hush el

Jeruf, opposite Birti, and await the boats there. Each party was to fire a rocket at 8 P.M. each night to show the other its position.

My brigade-major and aide-de-camp were to accompany me in the boats; all other staff officers, except the boat officers, to accompany the party on shore. Colvile was instructed, as soon as he thought it safe, to join the Vakeel at Birti, inform him I had received Lord Wolseley's orders to move to Abu Dom and take his troops with me, and request him to be ready to march immediately on my arrival.

These orders issued, I entered one of the boats of the headquarter escort Gordon Highlanders, and by sunset the three battalions were in bivouac on Sherri island. One boat of the Staffords struck a rock, and had to be abandoned as a total wreck. Arms, ammunition, and most of her stores were saved; no lives were lost.

A native who had hailed us from the left bank opposite Hebbeh in the morning, was brought on in the boats, and on being questioned in the evening, told the following story. He was one of the soldiers of the Mudir, and had been taken prisoner at Ambukol by the Shagiyeh, and sold to Haddai in the previous summer. When Haddai was killed, he was taken to Mograt—not to the island, but to the mainland on the left bank—where he worked for a man named Mohammed el Amin, a dervish. In the evening of the 25th, hearing the English were near, he escaped, and travelled by the left bank till he got opposite our boats in the morning. He said that at Shamkiyeh there were assembled Suleiman Wad Gamr with the Monassir, and Wad Abu Hegel with the Robatab, and many men from Berber under Lekalik, all under the chief command of Abu Hegel; that at this place the river passes through a narrow passage between rocks, and there is an old fort on each bank; that they had fortified the rocks with stonework, and occupied these old forts, and intended to dispute the advance of our boats. They had no artillery, and but few rifles, but they were numerous,—far more numerous than our force, — and had all either swords or spears. They had heard of Kirbekan, and knew that Moussa Wad Abu Hegel and many dervishes had been killed. They knew also that Khartoum had fallen, and Gordon had been killed. They told the people that Gordon was killed because he refused to become a Mussulman, and that the English, when they saw so many dervishes, would all throw their arms into the river from fear. They had heard, he said, of our returning; and when he left their camp the previous night, they were loading up provisions on camels, with the intention of following us.

On our way down, we saw signs of a hasty retreat having been made from Sherri island. There were a few native boats, all of which we destroyed, as we had done all we could find coming up the river; and there were some rough rafts. The whaler abandoned by Captain Peel on the 16th was found hauled up, and the stores that had been left with her were gone. Several natives were seen watching us from behind distant rocks, but we were in no way molested.

CHAPTER XVI.

RUNNING THE RAPIDS—BACK TO HAMDAB.

The boat officers had decided that it would be impossible to pass down the left-bank channel by which we had ascended the Sherari rapid; and accordingly we had turned out of the left-bank channel, and our bivouac on Sherri island was on a central channel between Sherri and Sherari, at the head of a rapid. In the descent of the river a different nature of channel had to be sought from that best suited for ascent. In ascending, wherever the river became too swift for rowing, passages had to be sought through which the boats could be hauled or tracked, and these necessarily were never in mid-stream, but always close to the bank,

26th Feb.

either of the main shore or of an island. A very great rush of water was to be avoided; and in consequence of these requirements, the passage by which the boats ascended a rapid was generally very shallow, and frequently only a narrow channel among rocks. To attempt to descend by such passages as these would be to court certain destruction for the boats; and the main point was to find sufficient depth of water, no matter how swift or turbulent the stream. Consequently, as a rule, the descent was in mid-stream of that channel which, in their upward journey, the boat officer had noted as most likely to be full of water.

I had originally intended to make the battalions in turn take the onerous duty of furnishing the rear-guard; but on considering the question, I decided to make the advanced guard and rear-guard permanent, chiefly because any other arrangement involving the transposition of battalions in the order of the column might involve delay. Having selected Colonel Hammill to command the advanced guard of Gordon Highlanders and the naval boat, and Colonel Green the rear-guard of Black Watch, orders were issued for the descent of the rapids in the following order — Gordons, Cornwalls, Staffords, Black Watch, commencing at 6.45 A.M.

Instructions were issued by Alleyne for the passing of the Sherri island rapid to the following effect :—

" The two boats of each battalion that are first passed down the rapid will not put into shore, but remain in the stream at the foot of the rapid, one near each bank, ready to pull to any boat that may require assistance,—an officer and life-belts to be in each boat. The two boats of the leading battalion to be relieved by the two leading boats of the following battalion, and so on.

" The first set of boats will be taken through the rapid by Canadian voyageurs; and a company officer will descend in each boat, who, on his return, should be able to steer a boat of his company down the rapid.

After the first set of boats have passed the rapid, a Canadian will be placed in every second, third, or fourth boat, as may be found necessary. At the hour named to start, adjutants of battalions will collect the voyageurs of battalions, and hand them over to Lieutenant-Colonel Denison.

"When the boats have passed the rapid they will be anchored on the sandbank on the right bank till that anchorage is full, when they will be anchored on the sandbank on the left bank.

"The life-buoys in all boats to be always so placed that they can be thrown without delay to a man in the water."

27th Feb. The rapid was run by all the boats of the column by 10.30 A.M., with the exception of the rear-guard and the rear boats of the Cornwalls, who were delayed by a boat of the Cornwalls which, in descending from Amarim, was wrecked above our Sherri island bivouac on a sunken rock. Her crew, arms (except one rifle), ammunition, and stores were saved. The boat was got to shore, but so badly damaged that she had to be broken up and burnt; and it was 1.30 P.M. before the whole of the boats were through and concentrated about a mile and a half above the bivouac of Shoar on the upward journey. The column then moved forward, well closed up, to the head of Uss rapid. Here it was decided not to attempt the left-bank channel, but to pass round the western side of Little Uss island. A sharp short rapid, with a nasty curve, had to be run at the turning from the left-bank channel, into the passage between the two islands; and the naval boat, which was one of the first to attempt the passage, struck heavily on a rock in mid-stream, in the swiftest water, and remained there. Other boats were with difficulty taken to her assistance by the voyageurs, her stores were unloaded, and she was got off; but in getting her off, a boat of the Gordon Highlanders got on the rock, and in freeing her, another boat of the Gordons was so damaged that she filled and sank. This accident to the naval boat caused considerable delay, as, while the other boats were engaged in rescuing her, and the boats damaged in going to her help, the passage of the rapid was blocked. Thus by nightfall only 64 boats, Gordons and part of Cornwalls, were through the rapid; and the force bivouacked in two camps above and below the rapid on Uss island, about 1000 yards apart. A few natives with spears were seen, but they all kept out of our way. We fired our signal rocket at 8 P.M., and were answered by Colonel Butler from the mainland, about two miles due west.

Our total wrecks this day were three,— one of the Gordons and one of the Cornwalls, already described, and another of the Cornwalls, which struck on the rocks and filled almost immediately after leaving the Sherri island bivouac. The repairing parties worked till late in the night, repairing other boats more or less seriously damaged.

The following day would take us into

the Shukook, where, if anywhere, the enemy would attempt to interfere with our passage. There were many places where the river passed between rocky cliffs, from which a few riflemen could do us serious damage. I did not for a moment anticipate that any large force would be gathered there; but I did think it highly probable that the enemy would post a small body of riflemen to oppose our passage, and that we might have to land a force to turn them out. Orders were therefore issued that two men would be in the bows of each boat with their rifles loaded and in their hands, and with accoutrements and ammunition ready. In the event of any shots being fired at the boats, these men were at once to return the fire. The column was not to be halted for mere stray shots; but should any serious amount of firing take place, the nearest boats were at once to pull to shore and land their men, the landing being covered by the armed bowmen. Wooden plugs were made and issued out to each boat to stop bullet-holes if required.

28th Feb. Previous to the advance on the morning of 28th, I saw commanding officers, and explained to them my wishes in case of our being fired upon, and of a landing being necessary. We then moved off, halting at the foot of the Uss rapid till two battalions and a half were concentrated there, and then recommencing the advance. My endeavour was throughout this descent of the river, as in the ascent, so to regulate the movement as to obtain the greatest possible rapidity consistent with power of concentration to meet any sudden attack. The advance through the Shukook was unmolested. As my boat followed the last company of the Gordons, I was in momentary expectation of hearing the first shots fired. It would have been so easy to shoot some of our men in the boats from the rocky cliffs, and to choose places for the riflemen whence they could easily escape before we could reach them with our infantry. But not a shot was fired, and not a human being was seen; and it was with no small satisfaction that we emerged from the rocky defile, and, having passed our old camp at Wady el Argu, ran the very nasty rapid intervening between it and the high Nile island camp at Kirbekan, which we reached at 11.30 A.M. This rapid required that every boat should be taken down by voyageurs, and occasioned considerable delay. At night the Gordon Highlanders and my headquarters reached Dulka island, and bivouacked there, immediately opposite the old camp whence we had marched for our fight, and the remaining troops bivouacked between the old Kirbekan camp and Wady el Argu. Our rocket was answered by Colonel Butler about six miles W.N.W. He was encamped on the north bank, opposite Birti island. We had got through the day without the loss of a boat.

While halted in the afternoon at the high Nile island camp of Kirbekan, the Gordons had taken prisoner an old man, dressed in the Mahdi's patchwork uniform. He gave no information, and next day I handed him over to the Vakeel, who pronounced him old and half-witted, and let him go. A messenger from Birti brought me word that the Vakeel had gone to El Koua with some of the troops, but was expected back in the morning. Achmet Effendi, the commander of the troops, was deeply concerned at our return, and begged me to let him know its cause.

1st March. On the 1st March, as soon as the troops had closed up to Dulka island, we continued our advance. We successfully passed the troublesome rapid above Castle Camp, and the swift water above Birti. I took Colonel Butler on board off Birti island, and dropped down to his camp, where I was joined by Colonel Colvile, who had seen the Vakeel, and arranged for his starting as soon as ordered to do so. The boats of the column pressed on to their rendezvous on the right bank, opposite the site of our old bivouac, where the Vakeel was now in camp.

The Vakeel, accompanied by Achmet Effendi, now crossed over to see me; and it was arranged with him that he should start on the following morning. There was a short desert-route from Birti to Jebel Kulgeili, but he preferred marching near the river, and keeping touch of our boats. Colvile now again joined the Vakeel's camp, with instructions to await our arrival at Hamdab. I sent off a messenger reporting arrival to Lord Wolseley.

Having rationed the mounted troops up to six days, the boats again moved on, and entered the Rahami cataract, where we were again obliged to place a voyageur in every boat. Each time that the nature of the rapids required this caused delay—as after taking a boat down, each voyageur had to walk back to the head of the rapid to bring down another boat. We had only sixty-seven voyageurs, and more than two hundred boats; so when only one voyageur was required for a boat, each had to make from three to four trips; when two were required, each had to make seven trips.

Headquarters, Cornwalls, and Staffords bivouacked on the left bank, about the middle of the cataract; the Gordons on a sandy island opposite; and the Black Watch, who had not yet entered the cataract, about three-quarters of a mile above.

The men were now becoming as skilful in the descent as they had become in the ascent of the rapids. An excellent system of leaving boats at important places to point out the route to be taken had been perfected by Colonel Alleyne. Boats followed at regular intervals keeping to the track of the pilot-boat, and the words "slower" or "faster" were passed down the line with rapidity. But we could not avoid accidents: two boats of the Staffords had to be abandoned to-day, and two were badly damaged, but repaired. Still, we had lost no lives, and but few stores.

2d March. On the 2d the advance was resumed.

Rahami cataract was successfully negotiated; and we entered the swift water at the top of Umhaboah cataract. Near our old camp at Warag we were halted, while Colonels Denison and Alleyne examined the river in front. Alleyne returned presently and told me there was a choice between two passages. That to the right was straight, but there was a clear fall of nearly three feet at one place. That to the left had no actual waterfall, but it was a rushing inclined plane, its worst feature being that the channel was narrow, and turned at right angles in the very worst part of the shoot. They had elected for this latter passage; but considered no one should descend it except the necessary two voyageurs (bowman and steerer), and the six men required to row each boat. All others were ordered to walk, and all arms were portaged.

The voyageurs walked to see the shoot, before attempting to pass it. They said it was bad, but practicable. To me it seemed as bad as bad could be. The channel turned to the left, and then sharply at right angles to the right. Just at this turn, two great rocks stood out in mid-stream. It was necessary to pass between them. The least error in steering would be fatal. To make the turn too soon would bring the boat on to the right-hand rock; to wait too long would sweep her on to the left-hand rock. Sitting under the shadow of a great rock, I watched this triumph of skill over a difficulty that to any one unaccustomed to such work would have seemed insuperable. Boat after boat came down at lightning-speed, the men giving way with might and main to give steering power; the bowmen standing cool and collected watching the water, and only using the oar should the steersman seem to need help; the steersmen bringing round the boat with marvellous judgment at the right moment. Now and then an error of half a second brought a boat on to the edge of the left-hand rock, and she rose and fell like a horse jumping a fence. But in the day's work only one boat of the Gordons and one of the Staffords were wrecked. Half the force bivouacked below this shoot at our old camp of Mishami ridge; half above it at Warag.

The Mudir's troops bivouacked at Kab el Abd, and we established heliographic communication with Colonel Butler at Shebabit. We had entered again into the land of the friendly Shagiyehs, and the first *sakyeh* we had seen at work since leaving Hamdab groaned out its creaking welcome to us opposite Gamra.

The two rear battalions were ordered to close up on the following morning, the advance of the leading battalions to be postponed till this was complete.

Early in the morning the passage of this rapid was continued. As one boat was coming through, her rudder broke; she struck a rock, and the voyageur in the bow was thrown by the shock into the water. He, fortunately, clung to the rock, and got upon it. A boat was lowered down to him

3d March.

by a rope from the shore by other voyageurs, and he was brought safely to land. This, and the length of time required for the return-trips of the voyageurs, made it half-past eleven before all boats were through, and in readiness to advance.

Passing through Kab el Abd, we looked in vain for the cataract that was "like the big gate of Semneh" as we went up. It had entirely disappeared. This was only one of the many striking changes in the nature and appearance of the river between our ascent and descent. The Nile evidently entirely changes its character at each place with its change of level, and no map of the river drawn at any one season can be even approximately correct for another season. We made good progress to the head of the fourth cataract. Here again it was decided not to attempt the channel to the west of Suffi island by which the boats had ascended, but to descend the main channel on the left bank. It was a long straight run of a mile and a half or more (distances are hard to measure when flying like an express train) of water broken and rough, studded with rocks both seen and unseen— a dangerous rapid to the unskilled or careless, yet safe to the trained eye and skilled hand.

As my boat shot down we passed the adjutant of the Gordons, with his boat stuck fast in the very centre of the boiling rapid—a useful beacon to the following boats. His was not the only boat that struck. Four others of the same battalion were on rocks. Three were repaired, but two of the five sank and were abandoned. The quartermaster was thrown into the water, and lost all his kit. The adjutant had a narrow escape for his life. Thrown into the water, as his boat sank, his head struck a sharp rock, and he was severely cut. The arms, ammunition, and men's bedding in his boat, and all lives, were saved. The Black Watch, also, had to abandon a boat that struck on a rock near Kabour. But by sunset, thanks to the admirable exertions of the men, and the skill of the voyageurs, all wrecked crews were brought to shore. All the Gordons and eleven boats of the Cornwalls bivouacked below the rapid, and the remainder of the troops above.

The Mudir's troops encamped half a mile north of us on the left bank; Colonel Butler's party on the right bank, opposite the end of Ooli island.

Orders were issued for the troops to close up below the cataract before advancing in the morning; and to Colonel Butler to march to Abu Dom, select a place and make preparations for his crosssing.

4th March. On the 4th the remaining boats passed through the fourth cataract with a loss of three boats wrecked, and, alas! with the first fatal accident in all our downward journey. The course to be steered through the cataract was a very tortuous one. The boats had to go from mid-stream over close to the right bank, and there pass between a rock and the shore, turning again to the left into mid-stream. Officers and a voyageur were stationed with their boats on the rocky islands to show the direction to be taken, but unfortunately a boat stuck across the stream, in the narrow channel near the right bank, blocking it. Instead of the remaining boats being turned in to the bank to wait till the channel was clear, they were by some error directed off into mid-stream, and the greater part of the boats of three battalions shot over a fall of about three feet, like a Thames weir in flood. That only one accident occurred is marvellous. One boat having safely shot the weir, through some error in steering struck a rock violently, and upset. Unfortunately she had in her two wounded men, both of whom, with a sergeant, were drowned. One of the wounded men, private Barber, had been specially distinguished by his gallant conduct at Kirbekan. A wounded private of the Black Watch also died on board his boat in passing through the cataract. His leg had been amputated above the knee, and it was an almost hopeless case.

It was nearly noon before the running of this rapid was complete, and we then moved down the river. A halt was made at Jebel Kulgeili, to concentrate two battalions, and the advance was continued to Hamdab, where three and a half battalions concentrated in bivouac. The rear-guard half-battalion Black Watch, with two damaged boats of the Staffords and six of the Cornwalls, were still in rear.

The Mudir's troops bivouacked at Dugiyet; the mounted troops at Kasingar, opposite Belal.

We had descended in nine days what it had taken us thirty-one days to ascend.

CHAPTER XVII.

THE BREAK-UP OF THE COLUMN—BACK TO KORTI.

At Hamdab I received a telegram from Korti. General Buller's name at the head was sufficient to tell us the retreat had been safely accomplished from Abu Klea. The telegram directed me to leave Colonel Butler in command at Abu Dom with the Black Watch, a troop of Hussars, the Egyptian camel corps, two guns of the Egyptian battery, a detachment of Engineers, and a hundred transport camels, with all the rations I could spare, and to bring the rest of the column to Korti.

On the morning of the 5th we moved 5th March. on to Abu Dom. The rapid water between

Hamdab and Belal offered no difficulty of importance, and by 12.30 P.M. two battalions had closed up, and the mounted troops had reached the right bank at Merawi. At 1.40 P.M., after the men's dinners, the boats of the Gordons and Staffords commenced to take across the animals and their loads, and by sunset the greater number of them were across, and all the infantry in bivouac together.

The Mudir's troops I had halted at Duaim, three miles short of Abu Dom. Orders arrived for them to be sent to hold Hamdab, for which place, on my recommendation, Dugiyet was afterwards substituted, as being nearer the supplies of Belal, and at the entrance of the Berber road.

6th March. The early part of the 6th was occupied in ferrying across the remainder of the animals, and in the transfer of supplies from the regiments going to Korti to the commissariat officer detailed to remain at Abu Dom. A committee consisting of Colonel Butler, Colonel Alleyne, Lieutenant-Colonel

Colvile, Major Slade, Captain Courtenay, and Lieutenant Colborne, met and went over the survey together, deciding upon the names of the various cataracts, islands, villages, hills, and districts through which we had passed. This was no easy task, as the same places seem to be known by many different names; and when the sound of a name was agreed upon, it was no easy matter to spell the word. Major Colborne's map, attached to this volume, represents the fruit of their joint revision.

A violent dust-storm blew throughout the day, but dropped towards evening; and at five o'clock I held a review of the River Column—the first and the last time it was ever inspected on parade. The horses, though their feet were tender from want of shoes, did not show any other signs of unfitness. The camels of the camel corps and battery seemed none the worse for their crossing. Two thousand of the finest fighting men that it ever was any man's lot to command were inspected in line, marched past, re-formed in line of quarter-columns, and advanced in review order. Having said a few farewell words to commanding officers, I bade the column, as "The River Column," good-bye.

The voyageurs were drawn up at the flag-staff under command of Lieutenant-Colonel Denison. Out of the contingent of 377 men that left Canada, ten had died, six of whom had been drowned in the Nile. Their six months' engagement expiring on 9th March, eighty-nine of them had re-engaged, and sixty-seven of those had ascended the Nile with the River Column. Without them, the ascent of the river, if not impossible, would have been far slower, and attended with far greater loss of life. Without them, the descent of the river would have been impossible. Officers and men, they had worked with unceasing energy and a complete disregard of danger.

The Vakeel had been met at Duaim by an order for him at once to hand over his duties to Izzedin Bey, and to consider himself dismissed. Another commander was also being sent up to replace Achmet Effendi. Both these acts appear to have been the Mudir's own, without reference to Lord Wolseley. The first, the dismissal of the Vakeel, was beyond his powers; and the Vakeel was reinstated later, and sent to replace the Mudir himself at Dongola. As soon as he saw that the English were really strong and in earnest, he had done his best to help us. I had no fault to find with him, or with Achmet Effendi, and I publicly thanked them on the parade, at which they both were present.

Achmet Effendi, however, expressed strong objections to being sent to garrison Dugiyet. The fact was, that information had arrived that the enemy reoccupied Birti the day after the Mudir's troops left it. Rumour exaggerated their numbers; and a force of 6000 men was said to be there under Lekalik, Suleiman Wad Gamr, and Abu Hegel, while an army under Mohammed El Kheir was said to be advancing from Berber by the river to join them.

7th to 8th March.

On the morning of the 7th, having said good-bye to Butler and his troops, I started with the boats, and early on the 8th handed over my command at Korti. The River Column then ceased to exist.

In justice to those on whom the great burden of the work fell, I will end this narrative with the last paragraph of my final report to Lord Wolseley: "I cannot," I said, "close this report without dwelling upon the splendid behaviour of the regimental officers, non-commissioned officers, and men of this column. The life of the men has been one of incessant toil from the first to the last day of the expedition. In ragged clothing, scarred and blistered by the sun and rough work, they have worked with constant cheerfulness and unceasing energy. Their discipline has been beyond reproach; and I do not hesitate to say that no finer, more gallant, or more trustworthy body of men ever served the Queen than those I have had the honour to command in the River Column."

THE END.

PRINTED BY WILLIAM BLACKWOOD AND SONS

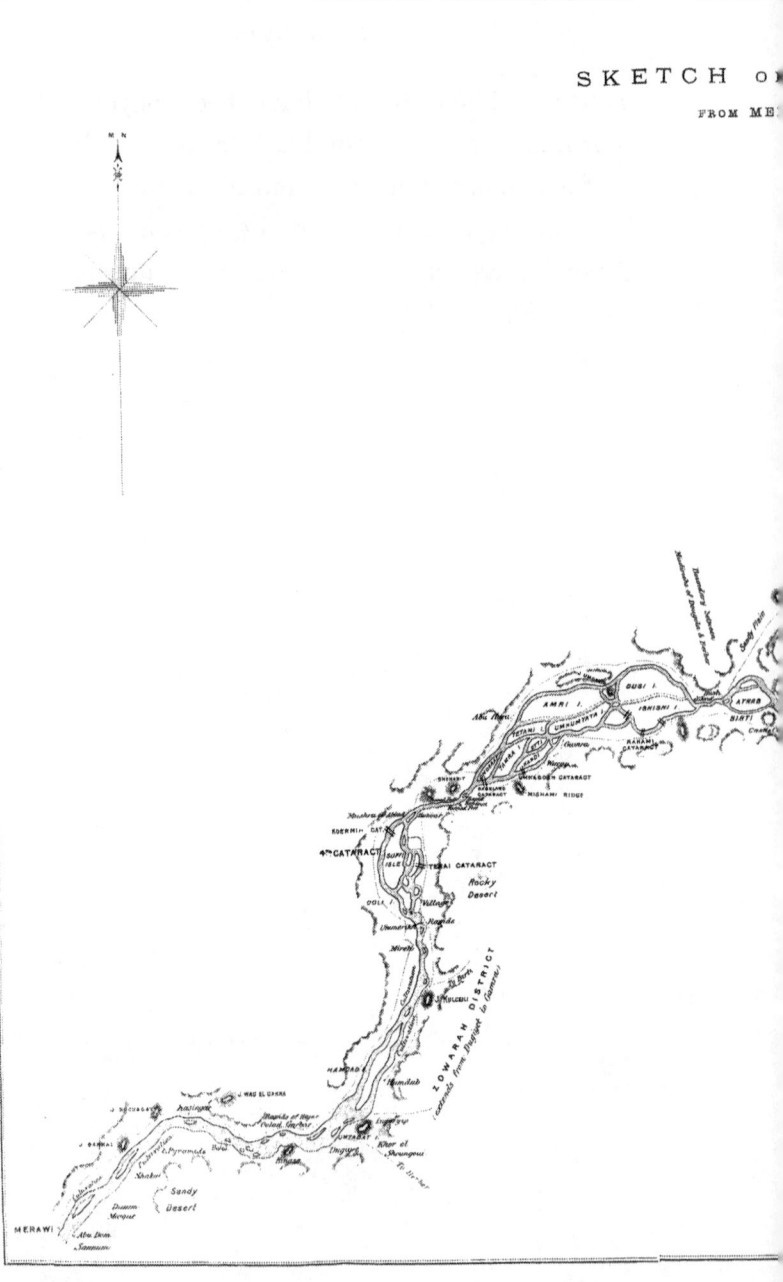

RIVER NILE
to HUELLA

Yellow Sandy Desert
HUELLA

Gray Rocky Desert

ELKAB

Yellow Sandy Desert

Gray Rocky Desert

HEDGEH

SULIMANIYEH DISTRICT

Yellow Sandy Desert

SHERRI ISLE
SALAMAT
HASMA

Gray Rocky Desert

Yellow Sandy Desert

SHERRI CATARACT

Black Rocky Desert

CATARACT

Black Rocky Desert

> Marks Action of Kirbekan.
---- Denotes Flank March.

SCALE 4 MILES TO 1 INCH

Frank Colborne Capt.
R. J. Kifles

www.ingramcontent.com/pod-product-compliance
Lightning Source LLC
Chambersburg PA
CBHW031134160426
43193CB00008B/138